# Groundwork 29

## BOOKS, BALL & BEYOND

JBR Publishing
113 Racine Ct
Monticello, NY 12701

Copyright 2021
Judith Brittany Wallace

Book Packaging by Earl Cox & Associates
Editorial Services provided by Aziza Read

ISBN (10-Digit): 1-932450-27-0
ISBN (13-Digit): 978-1-932450-27-9


Printed in the USA

# Dedication

To my parents, Allan Ray and Larnel Ray,
thank you for choosing me to be your daughter!!

# Groundwork

## BOOKS, BALL & BEY

JUDITH BRITTANY WALLACE

# Foreword

## By C. Vivian Stringer

## Books – Ball - Beyond

Judith Brittany Wallace was a member of the Rutgers University women's basketball team during 2006-2010. I was very blessed to have the opportunity to coach her. Brittany, was the epitome of a student-athlete, was an excellent role model and teammate. During her career at Rutgers, and currently as an active alum, she is a wonderful advocate for Rutgers University and provides a positive impact in the communities she is involved in. If someone asked me in a few short words, what makes Brittany so special and successful, they would be work ethic, hard work, passion and desire.

I always tell my players that hard work is the key to success in anything that you do. It does not matter where you come from, but where you are going. All my players will tell you, I never mind if you screw up, miss a defensive assignment, make a turnover, etc. as long as I can see you are playing extremely hard and with great intensity.

Brittany came to Rutgers with a strong work ethic, already instilled in her thru her family upbringing. Her family developed the characteristics of hard work, passion and desire in her and it was reinforced thru her father's coaching and watching her older brother, Allan Ray III practicing and working on his game. Throughout her entire life...academically, athletically and throughout her professional career...Brittany's tremendous work ethic and work hard has positively influenced others and has carried her to great heights.

**Books...Academically:**

Brittany had always wanted to be a doctor, ever since she was seven years old when she watched the entire birth of younger brother Aaron. Her interest in medicine ranged from pediatrics to orthopedics to nutrition. During Rutgers recruitment of Brittany, I was excited that she wanted to enter the medical field and I assured her and her parents that we would do everything to help her realize this dream.

As a biological science major at Rutgers, there we several academic semesters during her career, that I adjusted the team's practice schedule to adapt to Brittany's class schedule because of early morning science classes and lab offerings. By adjusting, we practiced at the crack of dawn from 6:00-9:00am. Her teammates were supportive of Brittany's desire to be a doctor and admired her commitment to this field of study. Brittany would offer her teammates advice on nutrition and eating habits, and once on a plane ride home, one of her teammates got sick, and they joked that Brittany would know what was wrong, she was almost a doctor.

**Ball...Athletically:**

Brittany was not tall or overly athletic for a Division I athlete. She did not have quick feet, was a decent ball handler and possessed an unorthodox, ugly shot form. Since Brittany understood from a very early age she was not fast, she knew she needed to get her shot off quickly and her shot form developed as a way to compensate for facing quicker defenders. Nicknamed "Chicken" by one of my assistant coaches, because of her jump shot's awkward follow thru, elbow sticks out half-bent and the ball spins sideways. Brittany perfected her imperfect shot thru hard work and consistency.

Her father gave up trying to change her form. I fought the urge to improve her fundamental shooting form as well. The old adage, if it's not broke, don't fix it. All that I knew was Brittany was a proven shooter! Instead, I asked Brittany to focus on improving other areas of her game – conditioning, strength, being a smart and efficient player, utilizing proper footwork, getting a lift on her shot, developing the ability to use/ read/come off screens and shoot. Everything my coaching staff asked of Brittany, she set about refining and improving, and all the while...leaving her shot form alone. Brittany maximized the most out of her basketball abilities thru hard work and dedication.

With tremendous respect, opponents scouting reports would say and team benches would yell: Brittany Ray/# 35 ... shooter, shooter, shooter!

As I look back on Brittany's basketball career and how it evolved, I just smile and am so proud of her on numerous levels. Early in her career she was the quiet player spotting up on the wings and baseline corners, shooting the ball consistently with high percentages. Later in her senior year, as a vocal team captain she carried the team offensively and emerged as the team's leading scorer. Brittany closed her Rutgers career, second in the Rutgers record book in three-pointers made (189) and third in three-point field goal accuracy (38.2 percent). She became the 29th player in Rutgers women's basketball history to score 1,000 points, even with her funky shot.

**Beyond...**Life After Basketball

Brittany has always wanted to blaze her own path and stand out from others. She never let amount of work or sacrifices it would take to accomplish the goals she set for herself become a barrier or excuse for not doing it. Even after college while encountering challenges, disappointments, twists and turns, Brittany did not allow anything to deter her. Today, Brittany is a loving daughter, wife, mother, a successful business owner and author. She is doing what she loves – nurturing, educating and improving the health and wellness of people thru nutrition with her business, Smiling Bellies.

It does not surprise me that Brittany has written this book. In 2009, while still at Rutgers, she took up writing a blog for the women's basketball website and the fans raved about her detailed and insightful posts.

In *Books, Ball and Beyond*, Brittany Ray has shared her story of real life experiences, trial and tribulations, successes and failures. Through her mature understanding that life is a journey to be enjoyed, despite any obstacles that may arise, Brittany has stayed true to her path by being resilient in her work ethic and commitment to hard work in order to achieve success in all aspects of her life.

I would highly recommend any aspiring student-athletes, male or female to read, *Books, Ball and Beyond*, as there are so many "lessons learned" to take away from it. Inspirational and motivating messages that everyone – young and old - can relate to, learn from and reflect upon.

# Table of Contents

# Opening Quote

"HE WHO IS NOT COURAGEOUS
ENOUGH TO TAKE RISKS WILL
ACCOMPLISH NOTHING IN LIFE."

— MUHAMMAD ALI

# Introduction:

## Numbers never lie, #29

When diving into the world of sports, there are many sayings that almost all sports fans are familiar with. Here is one of them: Men lie; women lie; numbers don't lie. For those not familiar with that phrase, it's simply referring to the stat line a player gathers during a game. In this instance, however, I am not referring to numbers in that fashion. Instead, I am referring more broadly to how numbers don't lie in the stories they tell. In my opinion, numbers do more than just tell the truth about an athlete's on-the-court productivity; they also tell remarkable stories about the people who choose to wear them. The number an athlete chooses, no matter how big or small the reason, has a story. Here is mine in a nutshell.

My brother wore '14,' so I figured I'd wear the number right after that, '15.' I wanted to be like him, but not exactly him, if you know what I mean. In my mind it made sense, and as I grew as a student-athlete, I fell madly in love with the number 15. I used it for password pin numbers, in my email addresses that I created, and even wrote it on my sneakers as good luck to match my jersey. I was obsessed with 15 to say the least, but looking back on everything, 15 wasn't the number I chose. It was the number that chose me.

It may sound strange saying a number chose me, but in hindsight that is exactly what happened. Here's another example. When I began this journey to write this book, a certain number profoundly stood out. Initially it seemed strange, but over time, with a little bit of self-exploration, it made sense. That certain number was 29. I noticed 29 everywhere, in familiar and not-so-familiar places. On expiration dates, on license plates, on books, on roadside dinner deal boards, on movie tickets and so on. 29 was consistent and I had to find out why. With a bit of help from numerology websites, and searching deep within my memory bank, I realized the number 29 was a part of so many of the things that made a difference in my journey to date.

In fact, I realized that the number 29 has been by my side my entire life. Like with my basketball number 15, the number 29 chose me. The first instance was my birthday. I was born on the 29th day of February in 1988, a day that appears once every four years. The 366th day in a leap year. A forgotten day to many, but for me a day that makes my birthday that much more special to celebrate when it actually does come. This extra day represents my life and journey into this fascinating world. Next, my fiancée and love of my life was also born on the 29th day, a day he ironically shares in October with one of my closest female cousins. Then, I became the 29th player in Rutgers Women's Basketball history to eclipse the 1,000 pt career mark. Lastly, I wrote this book approaching and during my chronological 29th year walking this earth. I say chronological because if you really want to count how many actual birthdays I've had, I'm only 7 and a quarter. Funny, I know!

So, you get the picture; 29 is special to me for a bevy of reasons. 29 is my compass I've let it guide me in completing this book. I have put together an experience-based, advice manual for student-athletes to use as a reference on their journeys. The guidelines highlighted in this book are based on personal experiences that have helped me find out how I can make an impact in this world. Most importantly, the guidelines discussed encompass the lessons, principles, and meaningful stories I have learned over the course of my life as a student-athlete, professional athlete, and entrepreneur, transitioning out of playing sports, that have made a profound impact on me. I will share 29 vital pieces of information that have laid the groundwork for my success in each of my different ventures. It is my intention that, by sharing them, they may help inspire and guide you as well.

# How to Use This Book

N early every kid who grows up playing sports dreams of becoming a professional athlete. That was my dream. We dream, and dream wholeheartedly, until we begin to understand the reality of turning those dreams into achievable goals. We learn while participating in sports over time that as you grow in age, skill, and level, the probability of becoming a professional athlete dramatically lessens. This idea is further illustrated at the collegiate level.

Every year there are close to 500K student-athletes that compete in the NCAA and, despite their courageous efforts, fewer than 2% will go pro in their sport. So what about the majority - the other 98% that do not go pro in their respective sports? Why aren't there more stories illustrating the student-athletes who have gone professional in something other than sports? That is the question that led to the creation of this book. I think those in the majority need to be highlighted just as much to show kids that they can still win at life, whether or not they become a professional athlete. I took both paths and wanted to offer my insights and inspiration to the kids that will pursue this unique combination.

**Groundwork 29: Books, Ball and Beyond** is for the practical thinking student-athlete that has interests beyond sports and is preparing for their future to make an impact in the world. My intention is to broaden your awareness of the limitless possibilities and opportunities that sports can present to you. Many of the skills you learn in sports are applicable to life, and I felt compelled to share my experiences learning those life skills. Even more importantly, I wanted to offer sound and practical advice to the savvy student-athlete that strives to utilize their skills learned through sports to set up a fruitful future beyond sports down the road.

In athletics, a new year is synonymous to a new season so I found it fitting for this book to be divided into seasons as well. There are three significant seasons included, Books, Basketball, and Beyond, divided into 29 valuable pieces of information for aspiring and current student-athletes to use as references on their journeys. This book is a guide to the process and forthcomings of a student-athlete. To help you navigate, within each season is a series of anchors and compasses. The anchors are represented by thought-lines, which are questions, quotes, or statements hoping to provoke thought and awareness around a particular season. The compasses are represented by the words of advice or guidelines I've created that will help build a strong foundation for any student-athlete. BOOKS represent Season I: the role academics and education play in a student-athlete's life. BALL is Season II: the role sports play in developing life skills. BEYOND is Season III: the transition and transformation an athlete makes after sports are done. Use this information at your own risk!

# Season 1: Books

> "EDUCATION IS THE MOST POWERFUL WEAPON WHICH YOU CAN USE TO CHANGE THE WORLD."
>
> — NELSON MANDELA

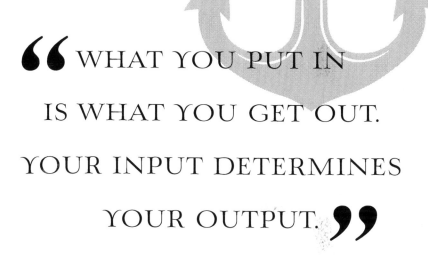

**"** WHAT YOU PUT IN
IS WHAT YOU GET OUT.
YOUR INPUT DETERMINES
YOUR OUTPUT. **"**

1

# HAVE PATIENCE WITH YOURSELF.
# LOVE AND TRUST THE PROCESS.

If you have ever played sports, or have dedicated yourself to any craft, then you've heard the phrase "Trust the Process." It's a phrase often muttered by parents and coaches to help their athletes understand that becoming great takes time. They say you must trust the process in order to develop, improve, and maximize your potential. As an adult, I understand that concept with more clarity than I did as a young kid. Initially, I did not truly grasp what my coaches meant, or at least, I didn't have a name for what they were talking about. I would ask myself questions like: What do my coaches mean when they say "Trust the process"? What exactly is 'the process'?

The answer became apparent as I grew older and started to go on my own journey as a student-athlete. I began to realize that what they meant is the very thing I watched my older brother live out growing up. I watched his process firsthand and often participated in it. His active dedication to becoming a better basketball player every single day was his process. His actions showed me that 'the process' required countless hours of physical training and conditioning. He showed me that 'the

8

process' also required a certain amount of mental strength. The 6am track workouts across the street from the old Yankee Stadium our father made us do in the summer was the process. I knew the process very well and reflecting on my development as a student-athlete, the process unraveled quite vividly.

In general, 'the process' is used to describe the path that anyone must take in order to truly achieve his or her goals and aspirations. It can easily be interchanged with other names that you may also be familiar with: the journey, the grind, the struggle, or even, the get-back. They all describe your unique path, your quest to becoming great at whatever it is that you do, love to do, or want to do. To go from average to good, and then from good to great, in anything is a process. Greatness does not come without struggle. Becoming great is exclusively reserved for those who dare to be fearless, relentless, and practically obsessed with their craft. Most people do not achieve greatness because they lose their focus and allow distractions to steer them away from their developing process. The concept of becoming great takes a remarkable amount of dedication because achieving greatness takes time and patience.

Patience has become so unknown in this social media age, an age that portrays success as instant, or better yet, an age that disregards the behind the scenes struggles. Social media, in essence, is a cover up to the realities of everyday life. It offers this façade that everyone is doing well when, in reality, that is not the case. Social media does not show the losses or the mistakes that you endure along your journey. Your process will reveal the good, the bad, and the ugly. There is no escaping the process, yet social media will give you the impression that you can be successful without it.

Going through the process is a part of every experience you will encounter in life. The concept of process is all around us. In nature, we see many different cycles that give rise to this concept. Look at the process it takes a seed to become a tree, a steady and tall one. That tree's development takes years to reach its maximum height and fortunately along the way the tree provides us oxygen to breathe. Look at the process it takes a caterpillar to encase itself into a cocoon, pupate, and eventually blossom into a beautiful butterfly; butterflies that help pollinate plants and flowers that are crucial to our food supply. Observe your own life and you'll see that too has been surrounded and consumed by so many different processes. Learning how to talk, how to walk, how to play an instrument, and how to play a sport all require their own process. If you are truly seeking the reward you want, you appreciate and embrace the process. Going through the process pushes you past limits you initially set for yourself; it allows you to see how much more you are capable of than you realized. It will be difficult, because anything worth achieving always is. In my experience, it usually requires hitting your lowest point to make it to your highest. It is in going through the process that makes arriving at your destination so much more enjoyable. Every single goal, aspiration or dream that you set out to accomplish will have a process attached to it.

Understand that this attachment is the development you must go through to acquire the necessary set of skills to achieve the task you originally set out to accomplish. It is the process of learning to see mistakes as lessons and not failures. The process of becoming the person you know you are. The process of sacrificing your time and energy into the thing that makes you jump out of bed every morning. The process of going through adversity to build and strengthen your character. The process of eliminating fear and limiting beliefs that stifle your progression and development. The process of pursuing your biggest dreams despite the criticism and negativity of others. That is the process

I am speaking of and felt compelled to write about. The process of going through life. A process that is overlooked because of our wide use of social media. A process that is not well understood by today's youth because we live in a culture plagued by instant gratification. A culture plagued by the mirage of instant success. Greatness does not come instantly. Greatness starts with a mindset that translate into actions. My parents, my older brother, and all the people who invested time in my development showed me things through their actions. Your actions are truly the measuring sticks of success. Your actions represent who you are. Trust that your consistent action is a part of your unique process that will lead you to accomplishing your goals. Let your mindset and consistent action represent who you are. It will not be easy by any means, but in the end it will be worth it and with that consistency may you maximize your full potential.

" WHAT ARE YOU
AND YOUR PARENTS
WILLING TO GIVE UP
IN ORDER TO ACHIEVE
YOUR GOALS? "

IT'S A MARATHON NOT A RACE. SACRIFICE
NOW TO REAP THE BENEFITS LATER.

I can not take any credit for anything I have ever achieved without mentioning the work my parents put in. My parents showed me how crucial sacrifice is to the recipe of success. They sacrificed so much it would be a dishonor to not give them credit for molding me into the person I am today. I witnessed their sacrifice every time they drove my brothers and I to practices, drove us to games, drove us to school, and all the other things that parents do. Putting together science projects, baking cookies for class parties, selling Girl Scout Cookies, selling candy for basketball fundraisers all center back to sacrificing their most valuable assets for us, their time and energy.

Learning to sacrifice what you want to do to accomplish what you need to do is not easy by any means, but it is a choice we must make in order to achieve our goals. Sometimes it's very important that we see the end goal as opposed to the current moment in time. Yes, we all enjoy having fun, relaxing, and hanging out with our friends. We would not be human if we didn't. Those are the things that make us happy. Sometimes, however, we have to sacrifice that happiness to get more important things accomplished. You have to see the sacrifice as temporary. If you stick to your main objective you will reap huge benefits. I'm sure my parents had their own dreams, but they put them on hold to do everything in their power to make our dreams come true. Through their actions this sense of sacrifice was instilled in me; sacrifice now so you reap the benefits later.

Through much reflection, I realized how temporary sacrifice went a long way, especially when it came to my education. Through my parents' sacrifice I was able to get a good education and explore things that piqued my interests and curiosities. Math and science, the very two subjects most people can't stand, were at the forefront of those interests. Up until college, I participated in the Roman Catholic Archdiocese of New York Catholic School System. I believe this was because my mother and father grew up in the NYC public school system. They knew that the public education system was flawed and would not cater to my or my brothers' needs as developing students. Historically, the public education system was not designed to allow black and brown children to thrive, or come anywhere close to maximizing their potential. My parents knew that and, therefore, put a great education on a high pedestal.

They sincerely understood the value of a quality education and, most importantly, understood its cost. I witnessed my mom work 2-3 jobs to provide for us, come home from those jobs and cook dinner, make sure homework got done, and so much more. I watched my Dad put on his train operator uniform everyday to work the night shift as I headed to bed every night as a young girl. I saw the sacrifices my parents made everyday to make sure my brothers and I had a roof over our heads, food in our stomachs, clothes on our backs, and love in our hearts. We often take the very people who stick out their necks for us for granted. These are the same people who put things on hold in their lives to afford us better opportunities in ours. Be appreciative of the people who sacrifice their most important asset for you. Time cannot be given back, so take advantage of it. My parents sacrificed their time, their dreams, and their desires to present me better opportunities then they had. They allowed me to pursue my passions and that's the greatest gift you can give any child. My parent's sacrifice set the stage for my and my brothers' success.

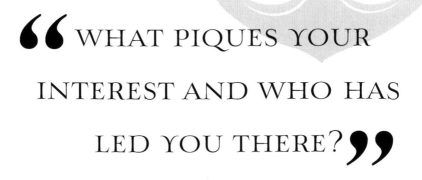

**"** WHAT PIQUES YOUR
INTEREST AND WHO HAS
LED YOU THERE? **"**

## OUR CURIOSITY IS OUR GIFT TO THE WORLD. EXPLORE THE THINGS THAT EXCITE YOU!!

O ur parents and, in many cases, those who fill out the rest of our support system, our mentors, friends, caretakers and more, are crucial influences on how we view the world as developing children. Our first line of socialization is very much rooted in their habits, personalities, perspectives, and opinions. Children often mirror what they see, and I was no exception to that rule.

First, I am extremely grateful that I lived under a two-parent household, a once traditional household in urban America. This may seem insignificant to those who are not urbanites but, for me, having both my mother and father present daily under the same roof was monumental. Where I come from, a one-parent household is standard. Single mothers take on the burden of raising their children with, nine times out of ten, no male figure present and no other significant help. Raising a child takes a village, not just one individual. The support of the village is missing in a lot of these urban communities. So, I am very thankful that that was not my experience and that I had a great foundation.

I was able to emulate two amazing people who I just so happen to call my parents. They provided a sense of balance and positive guidance for me all while consistently showing their unconditional love. That love at times was soft and fluffy, and at other times was tough and gritty. It was never anything extreme. Many times you hear of extreme parents pushing their children too far in an activity because they want their children to fulfill their unfinished dreams. I see it all the time; check out "Trophy Kids" on Netflix to get a sense of the level of extreme I am talking about. These parents push their children regardless of what the child actually wants, and that causes a lot of issues and strain on the parent-child relationship. My parents never forced me to do anything; they actually gave me an opportunity to thrive according to my own desires. My mother and father showed me two different views of the world under the same roof. I chose to pursue the things my parents loved because I naturally fell in love with the activities that they enjoyed.

Being under their roof was my introduction to the concept of duality, a concept I became very familiar with as I grew older. My father was the tough, reserved, and extremely competitive basketball guru that taught me about sports, and my mother was the big personality, kind, nurturing secretary who taught me the value of things far removed from sports. Before I ever even thought about sports, I remember books and a lot of them. My mom placed a lot of them in my hand. As a child she would read to me and when I got older, I read to her. She taught me the value of reading, an art that has almost vanished. My mother flooded our Bronx apartment with magazines, books, dictionaries, encyclopedias, and other educational book series. I would read about animals, distant places, famous people, sea creatures. You name it, I had a book about it. My mom also had the unique ability to transfer an idea from paper to an actual, tangible thing. She was the ultimate creative, and arts and crafts projects were frequent, even well into my high school years. We repainted ceiling fans, reupholstered furniture, picked out curtains, and so much more. She ignited the creative side of me, teaching me to be imaginative and teaching me to think on my own and, most of the time, outside the box. If I had a problem I couldn't solve myself, she always offered insight and often presented a new and interesting perspective I would've never thought about on my own.

My mother understood that self-education was important, and she showed me how to be independent. She always emphasized that if I wanted something, I had to go get it; nothing would ever be given to me. That emphasis planted in me the seeds of self-motivation and drive. She showed me how to take initiative by taking it upon herself to make sure I was being educated at home. She did not solely depend on my school curriculum to provide me with what I needed; she educated me on her own terms. She invested her time in my curiosity as a learner and honed in on it. Many times when we talk and reflect, she references stories of me growing up that highlighted my willingness to learn. She talks about me easily solving the block and shape puzzles she bought for me at 6 months old. I had a Pocahontas backpack I would carry anytime we would go out, filled with flashcards, also bought by her, in every subject. I knew I was a nerd from a very young age. My mom knew learning made me happy and she did everything in her power to nurture that.

I truly believe parents, caretakers, guardians, etc. have a responsibility to make sure they find a way to nurture their children's interests and desires. My mother opened the floodgates for me to seek my own interests by trying to figure out what I liked to do. All those resources she flooded the house with became my sanctuary and I read; I read a lot. I may have not read everything, but there was always something to read. I was a sponge consuming information. From experience and through much observation, I can confidently say children are walking sponges. They soak up information effortlessly in a short period of time, so why wouldn't you put them in a position to thrive in their particular interests and curiosities?

I firmly believe being curious is our pathway to finding out what makes us happy, the thing or things that make us wake up everyday. Our curiosity helps us to unfold our purpose, the purpose that each and every person in this world has. As kids, we dream and we dream a lot. We dream big without limiting beliefs; we have no filters, bluntly saying what's on our minds. Once, my nephew, at the age of two, corrected me for not calling a bug by its proper name; kids have no fear. Fear does not exist for children, because fear is something that is learned over time as we grow. We are curious about everything, and then, one day we have to make a decision to determine which way the wind will set sail for us. I believe we go one of two ways. Either we go down the path where we learn to weed out the things that are unimportant to us, leading us to pursue the things that spark our interests, or we go towards the road where we lose sight of the thing(s) that we love to do, replacing them with the things that we have to do or what society tells us to do.

The unfortunate reality is that most children growing up in neighborhoods like I did choose the latter out of obligation to survive.

"Survival of the fit, only the strong survive," are the words Mobb Deep uttered. Survival is a challenge when you grow up in an environment only fit for the fittest. Imagine growing up alongside poverty, not knowing where your next plate of food will come from, big bright lights always beaming on your building so you can't sleep, streets filthy with trash, in a

20

biased public education system designed to fail you. This is the tragic reality of most kids growing up in the Bronx and in any low socioeconomic community for that matter. Sadly, those distractions faced by kids living in poverty foster disinterest, lethargy and discouragement. The need to survive distracts them from pursuing their own dreams. They are consumed and suffocated by the harsh realities of survival and just like that are no longer kids. Kids growing up in low-income neighborhoods have to become adults earlier then they should. This is part of the reason why so many youths don't reach their maximum potential; they have to grow up too fast and take on adult responsibilities.

I implore you to hold on to your curiosity, your gift, and, if able, pursue it for as long as possible. If something makes you happy, pursue it, and pursue it passionately. Just don't forget to cherish the people who allow you to pursue it because without them, you do not exist. We may lose sight of our dreams; we may push them to the side or forget about them for a while, but remember that it will always be there. Hold on to your gift. The curiosity each one of us possesses is what makes us unique. It needs to be nurtured and channeled in a positive direction. Those who are curious about the things that excite them continue to be driven by that curiosity. They may struggle to find their way at first, but they eventually do. We all have talents and gifts that we can offer to the world. Be grateful when you are able to wake up and do what you love everyday. I appreciate my parents and their willingness to make sure I was fed, clothed, and, most importantly, happy. We may have not been financially rich, but we were exceptionally rich in many other things: spirit, hope, and ambition. My parents and my family were my support system, and I never wanted for anything besides a little peace and quiet. I had everything else I needed.

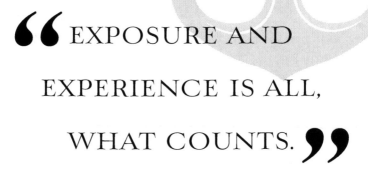

**"EXPOSURE AND EXPERIENCE IS ALL, WHAT COUNTS. "**

— LOVELY GOYAL

## EDUCATION IS LAYERED AND ABOUT PERSPECTIVE. LEARNING STARTS IN THE HOME AND CONTINUES IN THE CLASSROOM AND ON THE COURT!

Being from the city, you grow accustomed to the sirens, the loud gunshots, the barred windows, and the pissy elevators. At no point did I ever accept that those things were permanent. Those sounds and sights become familiar to kids who grow up in poverty as I did. Because of that, I often yearned for an escape as I grew older. Nothing topped removing myself from city life like time spent with my grandparents, especially my grandfather. Although they lived relatively close, in the Yonkers area, I was introduced to a life that my parents couldn't expose me to in the city.

Luckily for me, my grandfather TC preserved his southern roots from Macon, Georgia and afforded me the opportunity to learn about the southern outdoor culture. My grandparents offered me an escape from the constant noise of the city, an escape from reality. I have many fond memories of my outdoor adventures. What was most important about those outdoors adventures was the skills I learned. TC was a teacher by occupation and always went above and beyond to teach me valuable lessons. Fishing was my first class. Going out on boats, whether big or small, surrounded by the clear sparkling water, blazing heat, and thousands of bugs was serenity to me. Baiting the hook and learning how to cast lines always seemed novel. Waiting for a bite taught me patience while I enjoyed my nana's spiced ham and cheese sandwiches. I loved the silence and the peace that fishing offered. It offered me an escape from the otherwise loud, busy chaos of the city. I went from trash-filled concrete streets and smog to remote waterways filled with lily pads and fresh air that I breathed in deeply at every opportunity. This switch in environment made a remarkable impression on me. It opened up my perspective that there was more to the world than just the neighborhood I grew up in.

Fishing wasn't the only discipline I was a student of; my classes under TC also included art, technology and music. I vividly remember trips to the art store where I was introduced to paint brushes, hues of colors, and easels. I learned about the intricacies of oil painting, watercolors, palettes and canvases. This introduction led to me falling in love with "The Joy of Painting", a PBS show led by the well-known American painter Bob Ross. He was probably the first white guy I ever saw with an afro, and that was fascinating in itself. I was taught how to use a computer before computers were even popular. Our first household computer was a Dell, and *Oregon Trail, Jump Jet* and *Sim City* were my favorite games to play on it. We frequently had music class; TC sparked my interest in playing instruments, especially the piano; "When the Saints Go Marching In" was my specialty. He was one of my first teachers, and he was the standard to which I held other teachers. It takes a village to raise a child and my family was so crucial in my development. If it wasn't for them going the extra mile, I would have never had the opportunity to maximize my potential. He along with my mother were the first people I considered to be change agents.

I believe change agents are those who give, teach, and impact lives with great enthusiasm. They effortlessly translate their passion into their teaching arenas. I have been fortunate throughout my life to lean and stand on the shoulders of so many great people. I consider all of my teachers, my coaches, and every person who invested their time into my development to be my change agents. These everyday people made it possible for me to thrive as a student-athlete. Change agents are the people who will continue to inspire the next wave of talented student-athletes; they are the people who influence minds because they consistently show up, every single day. Change agents are the reason why I've been able to recognize and maximize my potential. I tried to learn something from each one I encountered, no matter how big or small the lesson.

Teachers are some of the most important change agents I know. They are the gatekeepers to our initial education, and, fortunately, because my parents made the sacrifice to put me in Catholic School, I had some very amazing teachers. My teachers were very involved and invested in me. Each teacher had a profound impact on my development, some more than others. My teachers were engaging, fervent, and visual. Most importantly, they relayed information in a way that made me want to learn. My teachers were the type to invest their own money to create opportunities in the classroom. I believe teachers have a tremendous responsibility to prepare children to want to become the best versions of themselves. It is critical for young people to understand that education is a basic element of success, whether you're a student-athlete or not.

Too often, growing up, I heard stories of so many talented and gifted athletes lose opportunities to compete collegiately because their grades weren't up to par. Something that they could control wasn't up to par. You want to play sports; you have to get good grades, period. My parents made that very clear. Trust me, I understand that school is not for everyone. My brothers made me realize that everyone doesn't find sanctuary in school the same way I do. That's fine, but school is a requirement for any aspiring athlete, so you have to get your work done whether you like it or not. That is the reality of the situation. Quite honestly, if you are talented enough to get a scholarship, how can you let something you can control (schoolwork) hinder you from getting an opportunity that every high school student-athlete in the country wants? Only 1 percent of high school athletes go on to secure athletic scholarships for college, so being a part of that 1 percent is special. We all know or have heard of the stories of those student-athletes who were supposed to make it but who didn't make it because of poor decisions and lack of guidance. The rise and fall of Lenny Cooke is one of those stories. At the time when Cooke was one of the best high school basketball players in the country, he felt his high school education was unimportant, so he dropped out of school and signed with an agent, hoping to get drafted into the NBA. He never got drafted, and he never played a single game in the NBA. His lack of education, guidance, and discipline led to his demise.

The point is that you can control your fate by doing your part and letting the educators do theirs. Clearly, athletes need to do their part, but one should also expect the same effort from educators. Educators ought to understand the seriousness of their roles as influencers. They are one of the first lines of socialization. They have a significant advantage of making a significant impact on impressionable minds. My grandfather set the standard for how I viewed my teachers and I believe the teachers I encountered upheld that responsibility. As a result, it is not surprising that I can remember the names of all the teachers I've had, spanning from kindergarten all the way up to my high school days. I can name only a handful of my college professors. In my opinion, because most of my teachers were women, their nurturing attitudes helped strengthen my intuitiveness. My ability to trust in my skills academically is rooted in how they groomed me. My teachers latched on to my curiosity and my desire to learn. Being a scholar should never be downplayed, and, in my case, I felt extremely comfortable being a smart jock.

School was an outlet for me, it gave me a chance to be a different person, it gave me a chance to experience duality. The idea of duality I found being at school was the same concept that I saw in my home in my polar-opposite parents, as was the duality I experienced in nature with my grandparents. My experience was the duality of being a fine student-athlete in an environment reputable for its violence and poverty. We live in a world of full of dualities, and, whether we know it or not, we struggle with those dualities everyday. On one hand, I went to a great, pristine Catholic institution; on the other hand, this institution was located in the heart of what society labels a ghetto. That ghetto, an impoverished community rigged with violence and fear, was a place that I also called my home. That was my duality. At home and in the basketball world everyone called me Brittany, and at school I was addressed by my first name, Judith. Brittany was the silly, laid back, humorous basketball player and Judith was the serious, focused, no-nonsense student. I was the same person living two different lives. As I got older and more aware of this, I wanted to dispel the dumb jock myth.

Student-athletes are some of the smartest people I know. I knew no other way than to do my best at my academics and athletics. I took being a student-athlete as a challenge, a challenge that many before me had already completed. It was a challenge I knew I could overcome because my older brother did it. I found great refuge in challenges and this situation was no different.

My teachers made it possible for me to see my own potential and encouraged me to successfully be both. They made it possible for me to aspire to be valedictorian of my high school class after just missing the title in elementary school. I lost by only a fraction of a point. So, I ended up with the salutatorian stamp and, man oh man, was I upset when I found out I didn't secure the number one spot for my graduating elementary school class. I was angry, but I lost honorably and to one of the most qualified students in the school. If I had to lose, I wanted it to be to the best, and, rightfully so, I lost to the person I was going head-to-head with, academically all year. Well, really, for 2 years in a row. Her name was Daly. Even though we competed in the classroom, we were still very good friends. You win some, and you lose some, so I promised to seek redemption in high school.

My coaches were equally as important as my teachers in making me think I could maximize my potential. They acted as my change agents outside of school, just as my mother and grandfather did in my home. Even though a school education is very valuable, it is merely one facet of education. The other side of education, learning about how to function in life, was their contribution. Participating in sports from an early age fostered so many great lessons for me that I still use to this day. The coaches I've had over the years taught me lessons that had everything to do with life. Yes, you develop a skill set from playing sports, but ultimately, you learn skills in sports that are applicable to life. Through my coaches I learned that paying attention to small details made a very big difference. When you are trying to stand out, your talent can only get you so far at the collegiate and professional levels. Truthfully, at those levels, everyone is talented. The problem then becomes, how are you going to separate yourself from a group of people who are just as talented as you? How are you going to stand out? The answer lies in the other qualities you display.

There are many intangible skills you learn from being a part of a team. Coaches can tell when players are not all-in, there are so many things they look at that it would almost impossible not to know. Let's begin with one of the most important qualities, your attitude. No coach, no teacher, no trainer, and, in fact, no one in life wants to work with other people who have poor attitudes. Negativity is extremely draining, and if you're a negative player, good luck trying to impress coaches. Next up, your coachability. Are you listening with your ears and eyes? Do you communicate well? Do you shut down when being coached? Every coach wants a player who can accept constructive criticism after making mistakes, not a player who makes excuses all the time. Then follows, your energy. Are you pouting when subbed-out or benched? Do you cheer for your other teammates when you're not in the game? All athletes must be willing to work hard, always give 100 percent, and show enthusiasm. Body language, effort, consistency, and persistence are all included in the checklist of qualities that coaches pay attention to and look for when trying to build their teams. These are the things that do not show up on the box score after the game, yet having these qualities is essential for a team to be successful. I've seen so many talented athletes not reach their maximum potential because they failed to recognize these qualities as important. These same qualities continue to be important when you transition into life after sports. You have to learn how to be adaptable and put yourself in the best possible position to succeed and, without my change agents, I would have never realized that. The lessons from all the change agents in my life, my family, my teachers, and my coaches, gave me a balanced view of life that I carry into the world everyday.

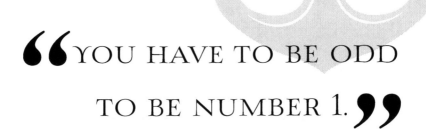

**"YOU HAVE TO BE ODD**

**TO BE NUMBER 1. "**

~DR. SEUSS

# 5

## ALWAYS REMEMBER, I AM A STUDENT 1ST AND AN ATHLETE 2ND !

As a Bronxite, specifically a native of Highbridge, which is located in the central west area of the Bronx, I grew up loving my city but hating its perceived image. I loved being from the Bronx, but I hated how the Bronx was always being portrayed in the media. I grew up in the former 16th congressional district in NY. The 16th district was once the poorest congressional district in the nation. I grew up in a neighborhood plagued by gun violence, drugs, and poverty. Despite all that, I still embraced my environment. I loved that it was a bubbling cauldron of culture. I loved that I lived amongst so many different ethnicities and cultures. The Spanish songs that come on in every corner bodega are in every city kid's blood. You can't help but enjoy songs like "Corazón Culpable" when they come on. If you know the song, you know it's one where you just don't resist the urge to move. The Bronx is wonderful in that aspect, but to people who are not from here, the other aspects are put at the forefront of their perspective.

Looking from the outside in, the Bronx is a grimy place. The Bronx is gritty; it's dirty and overall, is seen by society as a desolate wasteland. I am often reminded by my parents how bad the Bronx really used to be, literally burning. Rows and rows of buildings were in shambles; widespread use of drugs was in the streets; overdoses and death were everywhere. This was my parent's reality growing up, and, as I grew up, it became my reality. The Bronx may no longer literally be burning, but it still needs a lot of work. Our communities are underprivileged, crime-ridden, and devoid of inspiration. 38 percent of people here live at or below the poverty line. Still, if it wasn't for the Bronx, I wouldn't be the person I am today.

Growing up on 167th and Anderson Avenue made a monumental impression on my young mind. My apartment building was literally a 15 to 20 minute walk from one of the greatest sports franchises in the world. Living by Yankee Stadium helped shape my internal sense of excellence. Growing up, I would marvel at the massive structure filled with so much history; so many great names graced the New York Yankee jersey. How could I not marvel at it? I worked out at the track right next to it and the court right behind it every spring and summer. I could not believe that Yankee Stadium, home to so many successful athletes, was located in my neighborhood. The New York Yankees, also known as the Bronx Bombers, were in my backyard, and so they were my team. As is traditional in households, since my Dad was an avid Yankee fan, I became a part of that fandom as well.

The continuous excellence that I expected from the Bronx Bombers was what I expected for myself. I watched the Yankees win championships most of my adolescent life, in 1996 and then three years in a row from 1998 to 2000, with all the big names that everyone remembers: Tino Martinez, Chuck Knoblauch, Paul O'Neil, Orlando Hernandez the closer, Mariano Rivera, and, last but not least, the captain, Derek Jeter. They even won a championship while I was in college, and on that day I bragged and bragged about the Yankees and the Bronx. During those World Series in my childhood years, you could literally hear and feel the thunder of the stadium outside of my apartment window. Groups of cars decked out with Yankee memorabilia over every inch, riding down our block honking their horns and shouting their admiration was a common occurrence. That was the Bronx I lived in; that is the Bronx I remember. From the age of 8 and on, the Yankees' success made a profound impression on me. I grew up admiring that organization and yearning to be a part of a team that operated as one, a team that was successful and unstoppable like theirs. It made me happy to be from the Bronx. It made me want to uphold an "AND" philosophy: the philosophy that I can excel at being a student and an athlete with equal intensity.

Being able to be a student first and athlete second is not easy by any means. Some people even wish they could skip the school part and just play basketball. Trust me, nothing in life comes that easily. The balancing act that student-athletes take on is impressive, especially at the highest collegiate level, Division I. There is nothing wrong with playing at the Division II or Division III levels; that is the reality for some individuals, but most kids I know aspire to go D-I like I did. I decided that I wanted to go D-I early on, and once I saw my older brother accomplish it, I knew I had no excuse. I worked extremely hard to make my goal become a reality. I was not going to let my grades get in the way of my goal. It is a sad reality that many kids do not meet the necessary grade requirements to compete on the court. Luckily for me, I developed good habits in elementary school that carried over into high school. Again, my parents helped by emphasizing school as my first priority and putting me in an environment that allowed me to thrive.

Becoming first of my high school class was not easy, but along that path I learned how to manage my time efficiently and effectively. Although redemption was achieved, that redemption I sought after my loss in elementary school came at a great cost. It required extreme focus and a great deal of creativity to compete with the other students in school. I took it as a challenge to contend with the rest of the brightest in Aquinas. They kept me on my toes. Time management is one of the biggest hurdles you face as a student-athlete. You feel like you're on a see saw that continuously goes up and down. You are constantly juggling your academic life with your sports life, and let's not forget, the very little personal life you do have.

Studying and practicing were the two things I did the most. I was forced to become pretty creative with my studying tactics during the basketball season because I did not want to fall off the wagon. I'd study in the morning, on my way to school, as my parents drove me or on the BX36 if I had to use the bus. I'd also study on our way to and from weekend tournaments and on my way to practices. I studied whenever I could and by any means necessary. Studying, preparing, and more studying was the routine. During my senior year in high school, my family relocated from the Bronx to upstate New York and I had to commute an hour to school and an hour home everyday with my mom. That's two hours round-trip, and most would have complained; I certainly did for a while. Waking up at 5:30am every morning and returning at 8pm in the evening was exhausting, but I began to accept my fate with each passing day that I had to make that commute. I used those two hours to study, read, or even do homework. I valued my time because I realized I had so little of it to waste. Becoming the best at anything always comes with a cost or an exchange. You exchange time and energy for the reward of achieving your goal. In the end, I beat out the salutatorian of my high school by tenths of a point, bringing the story full circle. She, just like the young lady who beat me in elementary school years ago, is still one of my closest friends to this day. Yes, my teachers helped and inspired me, but ultimately, it was my action that made a difference. I wanted to do well and did everything I could to achieve that.

The pressure to perform on the court and the pressure to do well in the classroom are extremely high for student-athletes.. That is the responsibility you agree to when you play sports competitively during school. Balancing academics and athletics is a full-time job, whether or not you major in Biological Sciences. It's hard with any major because you still have to manage time between both commitments. Managing and allocating time in college is three times harder than it is in high school. Many people on the outside looking in have no idea what student-athletes experience on a day-to-day basis. I cannot speak for all student-athletes, but I can speak about my experience. In college, I was challenged academically by one of the most rigorous science curriculums offered at the school, and I was challenged athletically on the highest collegiate level by a Hall of Fame coach. This led to stress, on stress, on top of more stress. In addition to team practices and classes, where we absolutely had to be because we had class checkers most of the time, time management for student-athletes included a lot more activities under the surface. There were several other variables: team meetings, individual meetings with your assigned coach and with the head coach, random drug testing, mandatory study hall, mandatory tutoring, meetings with your academic advisor and your teachers, and any individual workouts you have. Let's not forget to mention that during the season, shoot-arounds, packing, and traveling that are piled on top of that. All these things are stressful, but that is the life you ask for when you want to play collegiate sports, especially Division-I. Balancing all of those activities almost every single day was physically taxing and considerably stressful, but that was still no excuse not to get it done. If my brother could do it, then I had no excuse. There are no excuses as to why you cannot excel athletically and academically. Academics should always be the higher priority if you are fortunate enough to receive a scholarship. At the end of the day, you will not be playing sports for the rest of your life. Less than one percent of collegiate athletes actually make it to the professional ranks. Making that one percent cutoff is extremely difficult, but, as a secondary option, you can always use your degree to open up doors for you. You will always have your education to fall back on. The discipline I learned being a student carried over into athletics. As much as I wanted to be great in the classroom, I equally wanted to be great on the court.

# Season 11: Ball

> EXAMPLE IS NOT THE MAIN
> THING IN INFLUENCING OTHERS,
> IT IS THE ONLY THING

**"DOES YOUR WORK ETHIC MATCH YOUR GOALS?"**

# DISCIPLINE IS KEY. YOUR ENVIRONMENT DOES NOT DICTATE YOUR DESTINY, HOW HARD YOU WORK DOES!

Having discipline and determination is integral if you plan on being successful in anything that you do in life. You need to be disciplined in order to accomplish your goals. I learned that discipline is the difference between being in control of your future and letting your environment dictate your destiny. High Bridge, Soundview and Castle Hill are the areas of the Bronx I grew up in. These neighborhoods are your typical notorious New York City neighborhoods filled with drugs, poverty and violence. Although deemed dangerous, these neighborhoods still fostered long lasting friendships, helped instill the love I have for basketball, and motivated me to not be a statistic.

As much admiration as I had for my environment, I refused to accept my environment as my permanent circumstance. I knew there was better, and I was determined to get out of that neighborhood and change my family's circumstances, either with basketball or academics. I remember walking to school in the mornings, at first, with my brother and, eventually, by myself with feelings of sadness because my surrounding environment was abysmal. There were always broken beer bottles and trash on the sidewalks. The entrance of my apartment building never had flowers, just small patches of grass and dirt. The brass bars and lobby doors of our apartment were frequently broken. Seeing people hanging out on the corner, in front of the bodega, listening to music, playing dice, and drinking liquor was normal. In my naïve mind, I couldn't figure out why people wasted time doing nothing all day. As I grew older, I understood that they were actually hustling. I didn't understand why flowers never grew in the courtyard in front of our building. I didn't understand why trash always piled up on the sidewalk without getting removed in a timely manner. I didn't understand, but that was my reality. My environment did not suck me in, it fostered the opposite reaction.

Looking at that those things everyday gave me the motivation to improve my situation. It made me want to be productive, and my parents made sure of that. I learned to be disciplined in blocking out my external environment and focusing on my work and basketball. Foremost, I was not allowed to play any basketball until my homework and chores were done. Every day was the same routine: I would come home, do my homework, do my chores, and then practice basketball.

Some people may not understand why you are so driven to accomplish a goal, and that's fine. Sometimes, people will not be able to understand your vision, and you just have to accept that. Just keep your head down and work, regardless of the naysayers. My vision was to make my parents proud by being a great student-athlete. The discipline it took to follow my routine became a habit, and out of that discipline grew determination, the determination to accomplish my goals despite others' criticisms.

My determination to be the best grew as I grew, and my mom heavily nurtured it. I regard my mother as my muse. She was one of my ultimate guides who has helped me see the bigger picture of things in life. I became very goal-oriented as I grew older and, for some reason, my mother always made me write down my goals. I still write out my goals, and I believe that looking at my goals every day helps me stay focused on them. My mother helped me understand that if you really want something and are determined to accomplish it, you will do everything in your power to do so. She also made it clear that I always had options; there was no set way to get something done. Everyone trying to compare his or her journey to another's should just stop right now. You're wasting your time! Everyone's journey is different. My brothers, for example, have all had different journeys to get to Division I. My oldest brother made his name in the CHSAA Class AA division in New York City and on the AAU circuit to solidify his scholarship. My two younger brothers competed in Upstate New York in the Section 9 Class AA Division. Kendrick became our first transfer of the family, leaving Quinnipiac to go to Kennesaw State University. Aaron was our first junior college player, playing at Garden City Community College in Garden City, Kansas. They all took different paths to get to the same destination. Discipline and determination played a part in accomplishing the goal of becoming a Division I athlete. My mom helped me understand that, and my brother showed me that, day in and day out, with his actions.

**"** WHO INFLUENCES
YOU? WHO MAKES
YOU BELIEVE YOU
CAN ACCOMPLISH A
CERTAIN GOAL? **"**

# FIND A ROLE MODEL OR MENTOR, AND APPLY THEIR LESSONS TO YOUR LIFE!

One of my coaches from college loved motivational quotes. Her love for them became my awakening to them. One of the most meaningful quotes that made an impression on me was, "Example is not the main thing in influencing, it is the only thing." That statement couldn't have been more true regarding the influence my older brother had on me. My brother was my role model; I wanted to be just like him growing up. My brother, Allan Ray III, is a major reason why I began my journey as a basketball player. His influence, along with my father's, changed the trajectory of my childhood. Before I even thought about playing basketball, I enjoyed being a girl scout. I was an outdoorswoman and loved it, just like I enjoyed going fishing with my grandparents. I enjoyed getting the pins and patches on my sash; I enjoyed selling and eating Girl Scout cookies; I enjoyed learning from the older scouts at our troop meetings. I enjoyed everything about being a girl scout, but then came basketball.

Something about basketball drew me in. It was the way my brother's eyes lit up every time he touched a ball. It was his high level of enthusiasm that sucked me in. He played basketball even when no physical basketball was involved. My parents didn't like us dribbling the ball in the house for fear of breaking things. The family beneath us was also not fond of all the noise it made. In any case, my brother just always wanted to play ball by any means necessary. We had a pull up bar in our Bronx apartment that quite often served as a basketball hoop. He would take balled up socks that acted as the balls and mimic crossovers, behind-the-backs, through-the-legs, and either run and dunk them on the bar or shoot shots from the bathroom door. The bathroom door was the official three-point line and the handle on the closet door before you made it to the bathroom acted as the free throw line. I'd sit facing the "hoop" and watch Allan do move after move, dunk after dunk, and make shot after shot. That was pure excitement for me, and everyday I became more and more interested in basketball. I realized that I enjoyed watching it just as much as he enjoyed pretending to play.

Day after day, I was getting pulled into the culture by spending time with my brother. He collected the Upper Deck and Topps basketball cards, too, and kept them in a huge binder. I would sit next to him as he put the cards into their plastic slots, organizing them with his own system. As he organized the binder, he would let me look at the cards and teach me the names of the players he knew. He knew a lot of them and collected a bunch of cards. Sometimes I would even take the binder from the drawer without his permission and look at the cards by myself. Flipping through the pages I would try to imitate the poses on the cards. A lot of the players had serious faces while others were posed with big smiles I preferred the latter.

I knew I started to develop my own love for basketball as my brother took me under his wing. I also realized the extent of my basketball knowledge was limited to my brother's made up one-on-none games in our apartment, pictures on basketball cards, and the Knicks' games we watched on TV. As I spent more and more time with my older brother, I began to notice that my brother and father would leave the apartment and wouldn't return home for hours; I was always at home with my mother. Now, I'm not saying there was anything wrong with staying home with my mother, and I enjoyed my time with her, but I wanted to go outside for hours, too. I wanted to know if the things Allan did on the pull up bar in our apartment were the same things he did outside while he was with my father. So, one day, out of built up frustration, I, a very sassy 6-year-old, had a major temper tantrum. I yelled at my father, explaining to him how it wasn't fair that my older brother went out with him all the time. I even accused him of not taking me out to play basketball was because I was a girl.

At that time, I had never seen girls play basketball, only boys, and I was convinced that that was the reason for his actions, regardless of his opinion. I was very emotional and dramatic, feet stomping, arms flailing, finger pointing, the whole nine yards, just to express my frustration. That highly referenced breakdown threw my father a little off guard ,and let's just say, with the added blessing from my mom, I was never left behind again.

My unofficial beginning to my basketball career started at my older brother's Saturday practices. I remember the first time I went to one of his practices. It was at the Gauchos Gym on Gerard Avenue in the Bronx. Looking up at the big bull's face blowing smoke out of its nose that was painted over the entrance of the gym was always exciting. Saturday morning basketball sessions then were run by Mr. Gardner Paige, a man who would be very influential in my life and in my basketball career. I remembered watching my brother and the other players shoot, dribble, pass, run, and, most importantly, have fun. I was so amazed at how good my brother was. He had an array of moves on the court that I had seen him use, or at least try to use, over and over in our apartment on the pull up bar. The crossover, the in-and-out, and the between-the-legs were my favorites. Out of all the fascinating moves he did, none were better than watching him try to shoot the ball. I had never seen anything like it, and, from that moment on, I wanted in.

I wanted to be as good as him, so I made it my business to emulate everything he did. I grew up going to all his games, studying all his moves, and absorbing his passion for the game day by day. Fast forward to high school, I remember watching him make the varsity basketball team as a sophomore. Freshmen and sophomores rarely made varsity unless they were exceptional, and exceptional he was. I am so lucky to have an older brother who always sought greatness. I learned firsthand what it took to perfect my craft by watching his every move. He motivated me to strive for greatness. As he was trying to perfect his craft of being the best basketball player he could be, I was right there watching in his shadow. I remember watching Knicks games on the TV, right next to him shouting at the players on the screen. I remember watching my brother be as devoted to his exercise regiment as my father was. He would do his pushups, sit-ups, dips, and toe raises religiously before we went to sleep every night. I remember seeing him wake up extra early to get to St. Raymond's, his school, to workout and play 1-on-1 with Julius Hodge before homeroom started. My brother's love for basketball made me fall in love with basketball. My brother's mindset to be the best became my mindset, and not just for basketball. Whether he knew it or not, he also had a lot to do with my drive to do well in school.

My brother didn't enjoy going to school as much as I did, but I knew he knew he needed school in order to play basketball. So, he made sure he met the required grades to do so. I remember watching him get his schoolwork done even though he didn't like doing it. I found sucking his teeth and shaking his head as suitable expressions of his disapproval of homework. In all honesty, besides needing it for basketball, I think my brother also put up with school because he genuinely loved to be a class clown. The most excitement he received at school was when he was laughing or making other people laugh along with him. Anyone who knows my older brother knows that he's a jokester. And for as many students that he made laugh, he upset an equal amount of teachers. He got in trouble a lot and suffered many times as a consequence; I wanted no part of being on my parents' bad sides, and I learned. I hated that he always got in trouble and made my parents upset; that made me want to be a little bit better. His troublemaker side showed me that role models are far from being perfect people; they make mistakes just like everyone else. They have flaws just like everyone else. My brother's flaw: mischief. I learned from his mistakes in school and capitalized on them. Having his influence around me helped me stay out of trouble and focused on my goals.

Your role model(s) should help you figure out a blueprint for yourself. They help you realize your potential. Up until then my brother and my father were my role models. Then later, during one of my brother's practices, Mr. Gardner Paige invited me on the court to learn the game of basketball. Mr. Paige would become one of the most impactful coaches I ever had the pleasure of training under.

**"NOBODY CARES ABOUT WHAT YOU CAN'T DO."**

~ GREG HICKMAN

# PRACTICE DOES NOT MAKE PERFECT;
# IT MAKES PROGRESS.

Being from The Bronx, the birthplace of hip-hop, I was practically birthed into a world of words, beats, melodies, rhymes and rhythms. On Saturday mornings, which my mom designated as clean-up days, incense would burn and music would play as I helped her clean. All types of music would play on our radio, from soul to R&B to jazz to disco. My mom kept me hip to the classics, while I learned about the hip-hop culture from my pops and my older brother. I grew up listening to my father spit Wu-Tang, KRS-One and Run-DMC lyrics most days. My father even resembled Rev Run when he wore his Adidas tracksuits and Stan Smiths in his heyday; there are pictures to prove it. I vividly remember my older brother rewinding his cassette tape over and over on our boombox to learn the words to "If I ruled the world" by Nas featuring Lauryn Hill. At every opportunity, I would sing Hill's part, and when her part was over I'd mimic my brother as he recited Nas' verses.

My brother was the ultimate MC and loved music so much that he conditioned himself to fall asleep with music on. For me, it was annoying and many nights before I was able to have my own room, I lost hours of sleep on the lower bunk bed because my brother had to play the radio in order to go to sleep at night. Anywhere from Lost Boys, to Camron to Biggie would be playing as I struggled to go to sleep.

Just to throw it out there, my fiancée grew up adjacent to Sedgwick Ave in River Park Towers, the same avenue where rap pioneer DJ Kool Herc created the first hip hop playlist and hosted the first hip hop party; 1520 Sedgwick birthed this revolutionary movement.

So you see, I am a product of hip-hop because I am a product of the Bronx. I am proud to say that the Bronx is my home, the Bronx is my heart, the Bronx is my life. Without the Bronx I wouldn't be who I am today. Integrated with my love of music, the cleverness of how hip-hop rhymes and lyrics, was my enjoyment of how words came together to tell stories. I fell in love with stories and that carried over into my love of reading. I am a voracious reader both because I enjoy it and because I learned a long time ago that most of the important knowledge we seek is hidden in books. My mom often reiterated that sentiment in our household. Furthermore, reading was another escape from reality for me. It allowed me to travel to distant places in the comfort of my home. It allowed me to be imaginative and innovative. I could come up with how the characters and the scenery would look based on the details in the book. Even to this day, I always prefer reading a book compared to watching the movie.

In my experience, most movies come from books and are more compelling in their original format; most movies don't even do the book justice. I'm one of those people who has to touch and feel a book as opposed to reading it on a screen. I love technology, but technology can be a little overwhelming at times. There's something about sitting down with a physical book that makes me more engaged in the story. It's something about the smell of the pages as you turn them that cannot be duplicated by a screen. I'm the type to read multiple books at the same time, a habit I picked up being a student-athlete, juggling academics and sports. For some reason, as weird as it might sound, jumping from story to story, subject to subject, theme to theme fascinates me as a reader. I kind of feel like I'm jumping in and out of many video games, but the video games are playing in my mind as opposed to on a screen using controllers. Trust me, I grew up playing many video games because I had an older brother, but books were always more fun to me.

Today, picking up a book and actually reading it is a lost art. Kids refuse to read and some even see it as punishment, but, really, reading needs to come back in style. Reading and listening to stories offers you skills that video games can't duplicate like developing a broader vocabulary and higher cognition. Reading all different types of books exposes you to lots of new words. Sometimes those words are difficult, like the Scripps National Spelling Bee words. I was exposed to a range of words and, as a dedicated reader, I always thought what's the point of reading if you don't know what the words mean? I know we all do this because even I fall victim to it, but we shouldn't skip over words that we don't really know and try to just figure out their meanings with context clues. Once I realized that I needed to know the meaning of the words to truly enjoy reading, I practically became obsessed with words: their spelling, how to use them in sentences properly, synonyms, antonyms and everything else under the sun. My best friends would shake their head every time I got the word of the day emailed to my phone from Merriam Webster's Dictionary website growing up; we were 10 at that time.

That was how I operated and learned; I just flooded myself with words. I highlighted words in books I didn't own, looking up their definitions if I didn't know. Then, I wrote them down on index cards to remember them. I strived to build my vocabulary daily and often focused on the words I added, but never did it occur to me that my vocabulary would strengthen by removing words. One of the first words I omitted from my vernacular was the word 'can't'. Removing 'can't' was initiated by one of the most influential people in my life, Mr. Paige.

He refused to let me use can't in his presence. I remember the first and last time he addressed my usage of it. I was having trouble doing a behind-the-back stationary drill, the same boring drill he made me do every practice, and I said that I couldn't do it out of frustration. He stood up after I threw the ball off the wall and calmly said, "Saying the word 'can't' is making an excuse as to why you can't accomplish your goal. You can do that drill. You can do anything you want. 'Can't' should not be in your vocabulary, Big B." That was the first of many lessons I would learn under his tutelage. Mr. Paige is known as the basketball guru in my home, he is the foundation from which my father learned and constantly built upon. My younger brothers never really had a chance to do a workout with Mr. Paige because by the time they were old enough Mr. Paige no longer was a coach. Nevertheless, they were taught his principles.

According to my dad, Mr. Paige's teachings heavily influenced how he trained me and my brothers. My father integrated many of Mr. Paige's principles and philosophies into his training and development. We learned how to play, but most importantly how to think about the game. Mr. Paige was one of my first coaches who made a profound impact on my mindset besides my father. He was a fair-skinned man with a long white beard. We call him "The Wizard". He was hilarious on and off the court, but when he became serious, you knew it. He was always blunt and straight to the point. He always made it clear that, through hard work and consistency, your goals can be accomplished. He made it clear that if I worked day by day, I would get better. He made me feel like I was capable doing of anything. His style of playing involved committing fully to your process. He warned me that I would have to accept all the territory that came with becoming a basketball player. If I wanted to be a basketball player, I had to commit fully to being a basketball player. He trained me just as he would have any of his other players, most of whom were boys. He made sure all the players under his tutelage played the game the right way. When I say the right way, I mean doing all the things that help your team win the game like making the extra pass, boxing out and moving your opponent back, playing defense with a hand always on the ball, and always looking up to make the best possible play. He made us critical thinkers by introducing concepts like the 3-man game and the diamond press. Questions were always followed after these demonstrations to make sure we understood everything he went over. Mr. Paige really loved teaching basketball, he never discriminated; boy or girl, as long as you wanted to play, he invested his time. Your time was his time, and he did not like to waste it. Mr. Paige did not let laziness or lack of effort infiltrate the walls of his gym. If you wanted to work out with Mr. Paige, you knew that you had to give 1,000%.

During his workouts I worked out mostly with boys and that helped my growth tremendously. I can actually attribute a lot of my basketball development to playing against boys, especially against my older brother. He never let me win, and, for a long time, I never scored a single point against him. He always played hard against me and made me earn every point. Playing against boys not only helped build my toughness, it helped me understand the tactical side of basketball, otherwise known as the basketball IQ. I realized early on that I could not compete against the boys' athleticism; they were stronger and faster. I could definitely compete, however, with their IQ's. While the guys moved at one pace all the time, I learned how to change speeds. Once I understood that changing speeds kept the defense off balance I used it to my advantage. As the guys used their leaping ability to put the ball in the hoop, I learned how to effectively fake shots and get my shot off quickly. I learned how to be aggressive and play with a sense of urgency. One thing I know for sure is that boys hate losing to girls, and once I stepped on the court to play, I had to bring it. Boys take it personally when they play girls, and, rightfully so, I took it personal when they assumed that I didn't belong on the court with them.

Hesitations and step backs rounded out the skills that made up my repertoire. I became more confident in my abilities as the moves I did in practice translated to the games. The first move I ever did in a game was a behind-the-back move into a crossover. I was 9 years old; all those sessions doing stationary drills with Mr. Paige finally worked after 3 years of working out. It took me three years to gain the confidence I needed to successfully use a move I learned in practice in the game and after that my confidence skyrocketed. Being confident in your abilities and skills as a basketball player is pivotal for success. Everyday, under the guidance of my father and The Wizard, I worked on my craft and dedicated myself to becoming the best. Yes, becoming the best. I was told you should strive to be the best at anything that you do in life because if not, then why even start. You control your future by the actions you decide to embark on. Work on your craft day in and day out if you have the means to. If you have the potential to become great at something, then why not maximize that potential? That was Mr. Paige's philosophy: get it done and be great while doing it; nobody owes you anything; everything is earned. My father took that concept and ran with it. You should too!

"EVERYDAY IS A WORK DAY AND A NEW OPPORTUNITY TO GET BETTER! HARD WORK IS EASY WHEN YOU LOVE WHAT YOU DO."

## TO IMPROVE YOU MUST DO MORE THAN REQUIRED.

## ELEVATION REQUIRES SEPARATION: HONE IN ON YOUR CRAFT, ESPECIALLY WHEN NO ONE IS WATCHING!

They say there is a fine line between passion and obsession. In my eyes, my father, Allan Ray Jr, epitomized that fine line. His fervent passion for the game of basketball also trickled down to me and my brothers. We eat, sleep, and breathe basketball because he did. My father taught me that passion and work ethic go hand in hand. He instilled in me a very strong sense of hard work. My father made sure that my brothers and I were not lazy. Most importantly, my father made it clear that we were not his friends; we were his children. We made the choice to want to play, now we had to work to get where we wanted to go. We put in work all year round, but when school was over the real grueling work began. My father sacrificed a lot of his own sleep to train my brothers and I. 'Til this day I have no idea how he did it. His turnover from getting home after work to waking us up in the wee hours of the morning was very quick. My father basically ran off of adrenaline most days, coming straight home from his night shift as a train operator to working us out at the crack of dawn. I dreaded getting that subtle tap on my shoulder most spring and summer mornings. To say that I enjoyed waking up that early as a kid would be a lie! I hated waking up that early, and many times I remember my older brother angrily yelling into his pillow to let out his mutual frustration right as my Dad walked out of the room.

At that young age of 10, I didn't understand the benefits of what we were doing. It felt like pure punishment, but I did it anyway because I knew my brother wasn't going to quit, and somehow, I knew it would make me a better player. As an adult, I've come to classify those 6am workouts my father put us through as the separation work. My father was very big on this work, the extra work you put in before or after your team practice, the work you put in on your own time. This was the individual work that was necessary to get better. It was the work you put in when nobody else was watching, not just the on-the-court training, but the off-the-court conditioning as well. It was the additional physical training, or the non-basketball work you incorporate in your training. This work will separate you from the rest of the pack if you stay consistent. Separation work is an integration of Mr. Paige's philosophy and my father's already established foundation.

For as long as I can remember my dad was always invested in his physical health. This investment is what I believe translated into an incredible sense of mental toughness that was shared between my brothers and I. My father was very disciplined when it came to the upkeep of his physical body, and in return, we valued the same thing. I remember doing laps around the track many summer mornings, and even late summer evenings, that seemed to never end. The track of choice was always the track across the street from Yankee Stadium. He would run laps at the track while I rode my bike around the smooth red pavement. First he'd stretch, then do a light jog, and then the real workout would begin: a continuous bout of laps around and around. I would ride while he ran, and I would rest as he ran. I'd always just want it to be over, but I knew I really had no choice but to wait. I believe running was my father's meditation.

Even more imprinted in my memory were his before-work sessions. Before he went to work every evening he would complete his daily ritual of physical conditioning. A short combination of push-ups, sit-ups and toe-raises were most often displayed. It never took him more than thirty minutes. He used an assortment of things to complete this daily ritual. Some days chairs and small stools were involved. Other days an old school ab wheel with a metal handle going through it and rubber handles was used. Pillows and mostly just the floor rounded out the workouts. The pillows acted as the cushions for his knees and back, and the floor was where the magic happened. It looked like a physical conditioning exam at a high school every night. I enjoyed witnessing this event every day. This discipline and foundation my father exhibited daily carried over into how my brothers and I were trained. We conditioned our bodies as much as we worked out in the gym, developing our on-the-court skills. My dad made us run track at Yankee Stadium just as he did, run steps in Harlem just as he did, do suicides and jump rope(speed and heavy) at Mullaly's Park just as he did. He also made us do push-ups, do core work, and later on, do leg and hip work just as he did. He trained us to be dedicated to our physical bodies with just as much intensity as he did. He made us understand the basic fundamentals of being an athlete, the importance of physical conditioning.

The physical conditioning is just as important as learning to use both of your hands as a player. It's amazing when I see basketball players finishing with their right hands on the left side of the basket. I understand that it is done to be flashy at times, but to do it because your left hand is underdeveloped is another story. If your left hand is hindering you from being most effective, why not just consistently work on your left hand until it is strong enough to do so? Why not turn a weakness into a strength? That's how you become a better player, when you think in terms of making your weaknesses strengths. That is how Mr. Paige thinks, that is how my father thinks, and that is how my brothers and I think. We play the game with high intelligence and great simplicity. My father's favorite phrase while training us was, "Don't get mad, get better;" I think he stole that from Mr. Paige. Every time I messed up a drill and showed my frustration I'd hear it. Frankly, I hated hearing it, but hearing it motivated the hell out of me. It made me want to give him a reason to not say it again. My father helped me see that certain things take time to develop. He helped me understand that your development is a process. Everyone develops on his or her own time, some learn early on and others blossom later. In the end what really matters is your commitment to your craft. It is in going through the journey that you will reap the most reward. You must learn to commit fully to the process in order to really reap the greatest benefits of your commitment. That commitment became my lifetime policy, and ultimately moved me in the direction of becoming a student of the game.

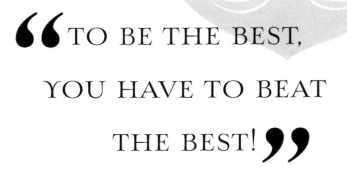

"TO BE THE BEST,
YOU HAVE TO BEAT
THE BEST!"

# 10

## HONOR YOUR CRAFT:
## YOU MUST ALWAYS BE A STUDENT
## OF YOUR CRAFT 1ST! WATCH, STUDY,
## AND THEN, DO!

New York City is and will always be the Mecca of basketball. No matter how far New York may fall off the map, New York City basketball always bounces back. Household names are made in New York City, names that will be remembered and talked about for decades. The players New York City produces are exceptional and you can find talent in each and every borough.

Growing up, I'd hear my father name-drop so many players that ruled the courts. He'd hint at popular names like Nate "Tiny" Archibald and Bernard King, who both were able to grace the NBA with their remarkable skills. He'd also discuss not-so-popular names like Earl "The Goat" Manigault and Ed "Booger" Smith, both of whom never maximized their potential. Their lack of guidance and poor personal decisions shackled their potential.

Basketball discussions were very familiar and frequent. My father and his friends would have nonstop debates over all things related to basketball. Some disputes were over players, who was the best, who never made it, who dominated the courts, and who didn't. Others were over coaches, their systems, their style of play, and their philosophies. A majority of the time, they were over teams, professional, college, high school, and even, recreational. Basketball was an around-the-clock thing for us, and it never stopped. Basketball consumed my life day in and day out. These conversations and arguments still happen today if someone sparks up a shouting-match-worthy topic. It's clear to see why I'm so biased to my opening statement; those players' talent and skill set speak for themselves. I am biased because I'm from New York, but I am also biased because I grew up in an era when New York City High School basketball was thriving and highly ranked.

My brother played in what I believe to be one of the golden eras of New York City high school basketball, 1998-2002. Big-name players were abundant. The older set of point guards that came a few years before him included, what some considered, the Holy Trinity of guards back in the day: Omar Cook of Christ the King, Taliek Brown of St. John's Prep, and Andre Barrett of Rice High School. The players that encompassed my brother's graduating class were good as well. Keydren Clark and Jason Wingate represented Rice High School; Curtis Sumpter represented Bishop Loughlin; Bobby Santiago and Ricky Soliver represented All Hallows, and the list of names continues.

Much of my adolescent nostalgia is filled with many memories encompassing the Catholic High School Athletic Association and summertime playground basketball. I went to every game with my father. I was a basketball junkie, and that's what I think it takes to be a well-rounded basketball player. Honestly, you should be a junkie in whatever craft you chose. When school was in session I'd watch my older brother compete on the CHSAA stage and when school was out I'd watch him compete on almost every reputable park, playground, gym or tournament NYC had to offer. First, let's start with the CHSAA. The largest Catholic high school league in the United States. It was one of the best leagues in NYC at that time. If you want to make a name for yourself, then you have to play on big stages.

The CHSAA covers a wide range of Catholic Schools located in New York City, Long Island, and Westchester. My brother chose to stay local and attend St. Raymond's High School located in the southeast Bronx. At the time, St. Raymond's High School was one of the premier Catholic, high school basketball powerhouses in New York City. St. Raymond's was led by Head Coach Gary DeCesare at the time. He coached at Ray's for 16 seasons while building an impressive resume. Coach DeCesare led St. Raymond's to New York City Championships in 1991, 1993, 2000, and 2001, and to state championships in 1993 and 2001. I witnessed the 2000-2001 city and state championships. During those days, the league was packed with great talent competing against the likes of other perennial powers like Rice, Bishop Loughlin, All Hallows, Christ the King, and Molloy.

My brother played his first year on the freshmen team and the next 3 years as a Varsity player under Coach Gary DeCesare. Making the Varsity team in his sophomore season was not a surprise to me because he played exceptionally well on the freshman team. I attributed his stellar performance as a freshman to those separation work sessions my father always made us do. Every game he played, I was right there, watching with my father. I am so blessed that I had an older brother that was very skilled because it gave me great insight into high quality, play-the-right-way, competitive basketball. Watching him play against all of the top names in the city, day in and day out over his high school career, made me want to do the same. The atmosphere of games at that time was unbelievable; the gyms would always be overwhelmingly loud and packed wall to wall.

I sat in many crowded gyms, packed like sardines in the sweltering heat, just to watch my older brother play. All I did was carefully observe and study. I became a student of the game. I believe watching those high school games helped me become a better player because I was picking up on all the nuances of basketball through my brother's games. These were nuances such as recognizing the crafty moves that made the crowd go "Oooh," seeing that high pressure situations for some, were clutch moments for others, and last but not least, understanding how to compete with a sense of urgency. The games were always competitive and never disappointed. The trash talking and flashy moves always kept me engaged. Julius Hodge was one of the best trash talkers I knew. One moment in particular always stands out in my mind. At a packed game versus Rice at the Gauchos gym I vividly remember Julius Hodge sinking two clutch free throws with almost no time left to seal the game for St. Ray's. He addressed the crowd twice; he talked trash before he hit the clutch free throws; and he talked trash after he hit the clutch free throws. His antics were hilarious to me, but, besides being funny, he taught me about confidence. His confidence in himself was remarkable, and he wasn't scared of the moment. I liked that about him, and I saw that same confidence in my brother. I got a chance to see my brother's confidence grow as he played against some of the best players in the city and in the country.

Now, the summertime in NYC is basketball junkie heaven. If you want to see some high quality basketball in the summer, all you have to do is hit up the parks, gyms and tournaments in NYC. In the summer, if I didn't have a game to play, I was either in the gym working out, or watching my brother work out, play, or do what I call tournament hopping. Hopping from one tournament to the next in New York was a spring and summer Ray family tradition. From dusk to dawn, my dad, my older brother, and I were in gyms, in parks, and at tournaments, getting our daily dose of city basketball. In the beginning, my brother would play all day, and then as I developed, the torch was passed, and I had games all day. My father drove us from tournament to tournament, gym to gym, and park to park.

Basketball was our life day in and day out. We went to all the hotspots throughout the Bronx, Harlem and Manhattan: Dyckman, Rucker Park, Kingdome, Gauchos, Rod Strickland, Douglas, City College, Kips Bay, Riverbank State Park, Milbank, Minisink, Abyssinian Church, Forest Houses, UDC, Castle Hill, and Hoops in the Sun. Sometimes we would venture further out to gyms like IS8 in Queens and Island Garden in Long Island. Mention any of these parks or gyms to New York basketball heads, and they'll know exactly what you are talking about. Mention my brother's name, and they will tell you how great of a shooter he was. Out of all the places I found myself watching games at in the summer, a few places stood out more than others: Dyckman Park in Washington Heights, ABCD camp in New Jersey, and Rumble in the Bronx at Fordham University.

I can tell you many stories of how my brother got his name "The Generator" at Dyckman Park! You do not become one of Dyckman's 25 greatest players without getting buckets and entertaining the crowd. Along with his partner in crime and best friend, Curt "Watch Me go to Work" Stinson, also one of Dyckman's 25 greatest players, Allan and the KYDA All-stars would put on shows at Dyckman Park. The most coveted scenes of the show were watching Allan and Curtis go one after the other and drop point after point against any defender. One game, Curt would have forty points, and Allan would have thirty-seven. Another game, Allan would have forty points, and Curt would have thirty-five. That was almost every game, and I honestly think they had battles between each other to see who could score the most points and who could excite the crowd more.

The park would go wild when either one of them got someone on the island. Now, the island is not a place a shaky defender wants to be. Getting someone on the island is another way to say to your teammates - move out of the way and let me go to work on this defender. Any time you hear "Iso!" and see a wave of the arm in basketball, someone is about to go one-on-one with somebody else. This isolation play, mostly situated on a wing or at the top of the key, requires everybody to clear and relocate out of your way. It's just you and your defender or vice versa. In this one-on-one situation, the offensive player makes a move to get by the defender; there's no help, just you, the ball, the defender and the crowd. Now, the crowd can either be your greatest friend or your biggest foe. That "Yeahhhhhh!" that permeates from the New York City stands is addictive and compels so many players to bring out their best one-on-one moves. Once you get drawn in by the crowd, there is no resisting temptation to exploit the defender. Allan and Curt put people on the island often. People running on the court, people in the bleachers shouting in excitement, and people outside the park watching through the gate set up the stage for Dyckman Park. I believe Allan and Curtis grew Dyckman Park into what it is today.

Now, Rumble in the Bronx was another goodie in the summer. It has long been recognized as one of the nation's premiere youth summer basketball tournaments in New York City and back when my brother competed in high school it was held at the Rose Hill Gym at Fordham University. Elite teams from all over the country competed in one tournament. My brother and his teammates on the New York Ravens AAU squad gave team fits. They were coached by the great Artie Green and the team was loaded: Francisco Garcia (University of Louisville), Julius Hodge (N.C. State), Curtis Stinson (Iowa State), Donnie McGrath (Providence), all played on that New York Ravens AAU squad. I was around so many talented basketball players and loved watching every second of it.

My brother graduated with the class of 2002, and being at the ABCD camp the summer going into his senior year was one to remember. The Adidas ABCD camp in 2001 was loaded with so much talent. As soon as you walked through the doors into the gym at Fairleigh Dickinson University, you immediately stepped into the hype with college coaches, spectators, family members and players all around. I'll mention some names, based on their positions, to give you some insight into the great talent that competed at the camp that year. The names that were all in one gym were unbelievable. Let's start with the top ranked point guards, which included names like Sebastian Telfair, Raymond Felton, Anthony Roberson, Gerry McNamara and Deron Williams. Representing the other two guard positions were names like LeBron James, Donnie McGrath, Taquan Dean, and Mustafa Shakur who dazzled the sea of spectators. Top wing forwards included Lenny Cooke, Francisco Garcia, and Top power forwards included Will Sheridan, Trevor Ariza, Leon Powe, Charlie Villanueva, and Steve Novak. Filling out the rosters at the center position were notable names like Kendrick Perkins and Chris Bosh. All day, the best of the best in the country were playing against each other. My brother ranked as one of the top players of that camp, landing the number 19 slot out of the best 50 at the camp. In addition to being able to see my brother and his teammates compete against the best players in the country, I was able to see my brother's hard work from our training sessions with our father translate to the court. His individual skills matched up to all the other guys at that camp. Participating in that ABCD camp in 2001 helped solidify his Division-I scholarship to Villanova. I was able to see firsthand that if I stayed consistent and worked hard, I could also compete with the best of them. My dream became even more real when my brother received his athletic scholarship.

" CRITICISM MAY NOT BE
AGREEABLE, BUT IT IS
NECESSARY. IT FULFILLS
THE SAME FUNCTION AS
PAIN IN THE HUMAN BODY;
IT CALLS ATTENTION TO
THE DEVELOPMENT OF AN
UNHEALTHY STATE OF THINGS.
IF IT IS HEEDED IN TIME,
DANGER MAY BE AVERTED;
IF IT IS SUPPRESSED, A FATAL
DISTEMPER MAY DEVELOP. "

— WINSTON CHURCHILL

# 11

## LET CRITICISM DRIVE YOU, NOT DETER YOU.

Criticism is a word that everyone encounters, but it's also a word that most people do not want to really deal with. Being criticized for much of my life is one of the reasons why I work hard in anything I set out to accomplish. I've been criticized for looking mean, for not smiling, for talking with a New York City accent, for being smart, for watching Jeopardy, the list goes on and on. I've learned that criticism is a part of life; you will get criticized no matter what you do. Truthfully, if I had listened to critics, I would have never accomplished anything. People will often project their fears, failures, and insecurities on to you to discourage you from taking your own journey. In many cases, the criticism comes from those who have never even stepped foot in your shoes. Be wary of those critics. Those people are all about talking and not about action. I advise that you steer clear of those people and view their projections as learning experiences. Do not let anyone or anything defer you from achieving your dreams. Let that negativity and criticism fuel you to not only prove them wrong, but most importantly to prove yourself right.

I learned that from my older brother. I witnessed my older brother fly under the radar in high school, deal with the criticisms put on him, and still make a name for himself. He was labeled as an undersized guard who could only contribute as a shooting threat. He was only a shooter and not a true point guard. That's what the critics said, and, boy, did he prove them wrong! My brother wound up ranking in the top ten point guards at the Adidas ABCD Camp that year. He finished as a statistical leader in scoring and free throw percentage and made the Senior All-Star Game. At the Bob Gibbons camp in North Carolina, he came second to Raymond Felton, averaging 30 ppg. Allan quietly showed me critics mean nothing, and confidence in yourself means everything.

As I became a more serious basketball player and relatively known in New York City, I began to become fully aware of my flaws as a basketball player. You become immediately aware about what people think about your game when you play in New York City. You hear everything even when you don't want to. You hear the criticisms, the insults, the hurtful words from the other players on the court talking trash, and most notably, you hear it from the crowd. I was not tall; I did not have quick feet; I had a heavy frame; and my shot was not textbook. I was aware of all my criticisms, but in New York City you have to develop thick skin to compete against the best players. The other players don't care about your feelings; they are trying to exploit your weaknesses as much as possible. They are trying to constantly throw you off your game and get you rattled. Your skills have to show up and show out, or you will get embarrassed. I never wanted to get embarrassed, so I always made sure I worked on my game. You have to believe in the work that you put in at practice and the work you put in by yourself.

As I grew more aware of my flaws, I learned how to block out the negative noise and focus on playing and getting better every day. I flipped that negativity into something positive. That negativity from the crowd made me want to prove them wrong and fueled me to become better. I worked to become a better shooter, a smarter player and a better teammate. I reiterate: I was not the fastest, and I did not jump the highest, but I knew I had a solid foundation of skills. I had heart, and I could compete with anyone. I believed that I could be just as good as my older brother, and that's what I strived to do.

I played most of my club team basketball growing up with the Kips Bay Boys and Girls Club located on Randall Ave in the Bronx. I also played AAU basketball with Abyssinian Church and Long Island Lightning towards the latter years of my high school career after Kips Bay no longer had a team. The Amateur Athletic Union (AAU) is one of the largest, non-profit, volunteer, sports organizations in the United States. Although registered as a non-profit organization, AAU basketball is a money making machine. The NCAA-certified AAU tournaments across the country pull in tons and tons of cash annually. Between the impressive sneaker sponsors marketing their brands to vulnerable young minds, greedy AAU coaches doing whatever it takes to get the best, AAU basketball players on their teams, and the owners of the extravagant facilities where AAU tournaments are housed, AAU is a booming business. Unfortunately, it's a booming business for everyone involved except the families of prospective student-athletes.

Don't get me wrong, AAU does serve its purpose. It's absolutely worth it to get the opportunity to be on some of the biggest stages of amateur basketball if you can confidently display your skill set. I was able to compete on a few big stages like Boo Williams in Hampton, Virginia and Top Ten Adidas

Camp in Suwanee, Georgia. At those places, you play against the best players in the country, get looks from the top schools in the country, and see where you stand against the best. All those are the perks of making the biggest investment in yourself in exchange for your time and money. The people who are most invested in you put up their money and time to give you a chance to achieve your goal. You get to see who your real support system is. You get to see who is going to financially support your basketball endeavors. AAU basketball is not cheap and, where I come from, money does not come easily. Honestly, the talent and financial circumstances of teams in major metropolitan areas are night and day compared to that of teams from the suburbs. Time and money are major investments when trying to land a scholarship that is not even guaranteed. These are the sacrifices made by parents, guardians, caretakers, and coaches to give their kids an opportunity to play on the biggest stage at the amateur level.

Teams from the metropolitan areas have to be a little more resourceful in finding funds to provide exposure for their players because money provides access; money is the primary resource that creates the opportunity to be seen. Teams and their families have to pay hundreds, and sometimes even thousands, of dollars out-of-pocket, just for a chance to secure an athletic scholarship for their players. Besides all the fees to enter tournaments, ranging anywhere from $300 to $700 per team, families have to take additional costs into consideration. They have to pay for uniforms, flights, rental cars, hotel rooms, food, gas, and admission for those not playing. Unfortunately, now, on the actual basketball side of things, AAU basketball has created a culture that lacks fundamentals and glorifies playing enormous amounts of games. Kids only learn how to play games instead of developing and learning fundamental skills surrounding basketball, both team and individual skills. That has become my greatest concern about AAU ball, kids playing way too many games and not developing their skills enough. The so-called developmental learning comes from watching games on TV and not the actual coaches. I am so caught off guard when every kid in the gym tries to shoot 30-foot three pointers when they can't consistently hit a simple 15-foot, pull up, jump shot. The priorities have changed dramatically; I blame social media and coaches who invest no time in their players' development.

Back when I was on the AAU circuit, things were very different. I only played on one AAU team (that loyalty that is no longer shown today) and I developed my skills with that team as I improved as a student-athlete. Playing with the Kips Bay Mustangs was one of the most beneficial things for me in terms of my development as a student-athlete. I became a member of the program at 8 years old. I started in a program called First Step. Every Saturday morning, basketball fundamentals were taught and book reports were handed in. "Books and ball" was the program slogan. That slogan always stuck in my head, hence the title of this book. The next year when I turned nine, I became a part of an organized team for the first time. David Nelson was our coach. He groomed my teammates and I to play basketball the correct way; we were fundamentally sound with good on-the-court instincts. Everyone knew how to use their nondominant hands to make lay-ups; we understood how to set up plays; feet and hands up, we communicated well as a team. I believe that was in part from our development on the court at Kips Bay with Dave and from our love of playing on the courts in our neighborhoods.

Although I am from the Highbridge section of the Bronx, I spent a lot of my childhood growing up by Soundview and Castle Hill. Both of my best friends, Whitney and Chantee, who also played on that Kips Bay Team, lived right next to basketball courts in that area. One court was located by Bruckner Blvd., called 174, and the other was located in Soundview that everyone called "The Jungle." 174 was located in a typical New York City playground filled with swings, slides and monkey bars, but The Jungle was a different monster. It wasn't the prettiest, but, to my teammates and I, it was a place to play ball and have fun. Despite it having two full basketball courts, we only used the half court that contained the only worthy rim to shoot on. The cracked concrete floors, the one slanted functional rim, the entrance covered with trees, branches, bushes, rocks, and trash made up our sanctuary. We would play basketball for hours against anyone who wanted to play. Most of the time we would play against boys in the neighborhood, or against ourselves. We were a team that actually grew up and spent a lot of time together, and I believe that's why we gelled so well on the court as we got older.

Dave always made us play up in age to help us gain our confidence as players and as a team. When we were nine and ten, we played against kids who were twelve and under. When we were eleven and twelve we played against kids who were fourteen and older. Playing against older and more experienced girls helped us develop toughness. In the beginning, we would lose a lot, and we would lose badly. However, we learned how to play as a team in the process. We developed our skills on our own and collectively at team practice. We built our team chemistry and gained our confidence. Anjale Barrett, younger sister of Andre Barrett, and I naturally headlined the team because both of our older brothers were making names for themselves in the NYC basketball community. Don't be mistaken we may have been the "names" of the team, but everyone contributed to our success.

Our coach Dave made sure that we played against the best teams in NYC. A lot of great teams and players played in NYC at the time I played. In Manhattan, you had the Douglas Panthers headed by legendary coach Hammer Stevens with players like Priscilla Edwards, Kisha Stokes, Yada Beener, and Vionca Murray. In Harlem, you had Abyssinian Church headed by Alexis "Lex" Smith with players like Sharlyn Harper, Victoria Sweet, and Isha Nixon. In the other part of the Bronx, you had Roberto Clemente headed by Cecil King with players like Tina Charles, Marissa Flagg, and Melanie Murphy. Also in Manhattan, you had Exodus headed by Apache Paschall with players like Epiphanny Prince, Erica Morrow, and Kia Vaughn. And later on from Brooklyn, you had No Limit headed by Coach Munch with players like Corin Adams and Kimberly Blakney. This was our competition growing up, and this was the competition that helped us develop and elevate our skills. The quality of basketball at that time was high because our coaches taught us the fundamentals and kept us on our toes with accountability. Fundamentals like being able to use both hands to dribble the ball and making layups are not common today. Screaming at a player because they allowed another player to drive the baseline and not cut it off is also not common. Coaches have moved away from the value of teaching and moved in the direction of just winning games. Find a coach that is willing to teach you. If you want to be a great player you have to master the fundamentals first. Your groundwork is crucial to how your development will pan out over time! Master the fundamentals, then you will have room to improve sound habits.

**"THE MOST IMPORTANT KIND OF FREEDOM IS TO BE WHAT YOU REALLY ARE."**

~ JIM MORRISON

# 12

## VERITAS

### YOUR TRUTH IS UNLIKE ANYONE ELSE'S, TELL IT UNAPOLOGETICALLY!

Have you ever tried to be someone else? Nope I didn't think so. I would like to believe that imitation on that level is only for the movies. You should always be striving to become the very best version of yourself, not the best version of someone else. Be yourself unapologetically because no one will ever be able to duplicate you. You are the flow and have always been, you just have to believe it. I've always strived to be comfortable in my own skin and be an authentic person. I've learned that comparing yourself to other people only leads to insecurity and disappointment. Your journey and another person's journey are completely different. Your story is uniquely yours and no one else's.

My mother is one of the most authentic people I know, and she taught me about authenticity just by being the person that she is. I've always noticed her confidence in herself. She has this aura about her, that when she steps into a room, everyone loves being around her; her spirit is always high. That boldness to be herself definitely rubbed off on me. The boldness to be myself was definitely challenged when I was deciding which high school to attend. Everyone wanted me to go a school that had a good basketball program, but I felt otherwise. When choosing a school, do not feel pressured by others' opinions, just use their words as advice. I had a vision for my life that no one else saw; everyone thought I was crazy for believing it. My brother won a state championship at a high school praised for its basketball superiority. I, on the other hand, went about winning a state championship in a very different way; I won a state championship at a high school praised for it's academic superiority, Aquinas High School.

Aquinas High School is a small, private, all-girls, preparatory school located not too far from the Bronx Zoo and adjacent to the well-known Little Italy on Arthur Avenue, a perk that I enjoyed. I often ventured to Arthur Ave. after many practices to get antipasto platters and gigantic fried rice balls, called Arancini. I consider my alma mater to be a gem in the depths of the Bronx. Aquinas will forever be imprinted in my being because of the long-lasting relationships I fostered there. Any woman who has ever had the pleasure of going there knows exactly what I'm talking about. The Aquinas community is like a sisterhood. The friendships that I fostered as a teenager with my classmates, my coaches, and some of my teachers are still very much alive today. Going to an all-girls institution may seem very strange to most young girls, but my parents wanted me to stay focused as much as possible. It also helped that my older brother went to an all-boys high school, so I really had no option to complain. Going to Aquinas was one of the best decisions that I made in my life as a student first, athlete second. The school represented my truth as an academic scholar. That was my main priority and exactly what I wanted, a high school that would prepare me for college, not just a high school I could excel athletically at.

At the risk of sounding prideful, I'm confident that I could've contributed athletically to any school I attended because my skills were decent and I worked hard, but I did not feel every school in the city could challenge me academically. NYC offers so many great schools, but I knew I belonged in the Bronx. The motto of Aquinas is Veritas (Truth), and that deeply resonated with me. It represented my truth as an eternal learner, and, as a Bronx native, I wanted to stay local; those are two of the main reasons I chose to go there. I knew the teachers there would challenge me, given that it was a Blue Ribbon school. I knew I could change and influence the athletic culture because a few of my teammates I played with at Kips Bay made the decision to choose Aquinas too. We knew we could make history by influencing the athletic culture of the school. It would be a challenge, but I loved challenges; challenges always make life more interesting.

During my tenure at Aquinas we developed and improved our skills a little more each year. Over my four years, my teammates and I established a winning culture on the sports side, just as the school established a thriving culture on the academic side. I made the Varsity team my freshman year and made an immediate impact alongside a group of upperclassmen; we lost in the city semifinals by three points that year. My sophomore season, we made it a step closer, losing in the city finals. My junior season was the same as my first, a loss in the semifinals. I was pressed for time, and, that summer going into my senior season, I knew it was my last chance to make history. I had just completed my second summer at Adidas Camp and gained a lot of confidence going into my senior year. I gained a lot of confidence going into my senior season for two reasons: competing at that big exposure camp two years in a row and working with a guy by the name of Jerry Powell, JP.

Besides working with my father, my brothers and I worked consistently with JP. JP, the friend, is a genuine, nice, and down-to-earth guy, but JP, the trainer, is quite the opposite. As a trainer, JP is very passionate about the game and very serious about his craft. If you don't like real criticism, then Jerry is not for you! His style is loud, blunt, no-nonsense. It's also quite humorous. He despises laziness and bad attitudes. He improves your weaknesses and capitalizes on your strengths. JP is one of the best trainers I've ever had, right next to the guru, Mr. Paige; he gets you the results you need to be a successful basketball player, hence his organization's name: Basketball Results. My father would drive us an hour to Long Island, just so we could work out with Jerry because he's that good. What makes JP even more credible as a great trainer is the way in which he utilizes his small space. As you pull up into the parking lot of Jerry's gym, you see big, white letters on the side of a red brick building that read "BABYLON TOWN HALL ANNEX." His gym is located right inside that town annex and is smaller than a regulation gym. It reminds me of my high school gym, actually, small and tight. On any given day, JP may have one of his pupils training a group of 15-20 kids on one side of the court while he is training a group of collegiate athletes on the other. Jerry is great at what he does, and training with him made me realize I had everything I needed to make my senior season my most impactful year. I wanted to win a city championship and a state championship, the same thing I saw my brother accomplish 5 years earlier with St. Raymond's and the very accomplishment I envisioned before I even stepped foot into Aquinas.

You see, that very day when my brother won the state championship in Glens Falls, NY, he challenged me to do the same. It wasn't a direct, verbal challenge from him; it was an unspoken, sibling rivalry, basketball challenge. If my brother could win, I thought I could surely win as well. To add fuel to the fire, my brother would tease me that I couldn't do it at a school that focused entirely on academics. Now, you know, I had to prove him wrong. I approached my last year of high school with a remarkable amount of urgency and focus. With a lot of hard work and a little bit of luck on our side, the Aquinas Lady Bears varsity basketball squad became a special team and won the school's first Class B City Championship and State Championship. I even remember having a special ceremony at the school. I went into my first year of college on a basketball high knowing that I could make an impact on a Division-I team.

**"** PREPARE TO BE
OVERWHELMED BY THE
RECRUITING PROCESS.
IF YOU ARE GOOD, THE
COACHES WILL COME. IF
YOU ARE GOOD ENOUGH,
THEY WILL OFFER. **"**

—ALLAN N. RAY, JR.

# TAKE ADVANTAGE, AND SEIZE EVERY OPPORTUNITY!

Deciding on a college or university is one of the most important decisions a student-athlete makes. It would be a disservice to every current and aspiring student-athlete not to advise you to choose wisely. As a student-athlete, it is critical to factor in every possible variable when making your decision. These are some of the things I considered when making my decision: Location, tradition, coaching style, atmosphere, culture, and academics. When making my decision to go to college, I wanted to be close to home so my parents and family could watch me play, so think about your support system if that is important to you. Keeping a great support system around you helps you navigate the ups and downs of being a student-athlete. Academics were a priority. Of course I wanted to be challenged academically, but athletically I didn't want to have to develop alongside a program. I wanted to go somewhere already established. It took me four grueling years to get where I wanted to go in high school, and I did not want to go through that in college. It's a funny story as to how I even landed at Rutgers University.

Choosing to go to Rutgers was a very late and abrupt decision, mainly because of miscommunication; I was completely unaware that they were extremely interested in me as a basketball player. To make a long story short, the summer going into my senior year of high school, my family and I relocated upstate to Middletown, NY. Our phone number and address changed, so it was a little difficult for college coaches to get in contact with me during that short period. Remember, this was before the social media age, so no instant updates on my whereabouts. I even remember when I got on the phone with a few coaches weeks after that move, they reinforced how hard it was to get a hold of my contact information. Coach Stringer was one of those coaches. She actually got my number from one of her former players and one of my future coaches, Tasha Pointer, who was recruiting me at Columbia University at that time. Funny, right? I was very shocked because I knew who Coach Stringer was, but I never thought in my wildest dreams that a tremendous woman like her wanted me at such a fine institution with a rich basketball tradition.

That summer I was getting interest from a wide range of schools: St. John's, Seton Hall, Towson, Penn State, Georgetown, Columbia, Princeton, Virginia, but not Rutgers. Now, the recruiting process for any student-athlete, especially if you're highly touted, is a bit overwhelming. I watched my brother go through the recruiting process first, and then my process followed. Letters and phone calls are abundant; unofficial and official visits come and go. If you're really lucky, the coaches make it a priority to make a home visit. I made unofficial visits to St. John's, Georgetown, Princeton, and Seton Hall because I wanted to stay close to my family. Truthfully, I was heavily leaning to commit to Georgetown because they showed the most interest and the most consistency out of all the schools recruiting me, but unexpectedly things worked out differently. I knew, going into my last AAU summer, that I wanted to make my college decision before I started my senior season, just in case I got injured, to assure my scholarship security. I also didn't want to have to worry about choosing a school on top of finishing my last year in high school with challenging advanced placement classes.

One of the last tournaments I played in that summer was the Big Apple Classic at Fordham University, the same gym I loved watching my brother play on. He always played well in that gym. I knew I had to do the same. Before every one of my games, I saw the Rutgers representatives, Carlene Mitchell and C. Vivian Stringer (CVS), sitting in chairs in the college coach section getting ready to watch my games. I was stunned and knew I had to seize my opportunity to play well. One of those games was against big name, Danielle Wilson, from Long Island. I played hard that game, and even though we lost, I made a big impression scoring 30+. I had a few more games like that during that tournament. After my performance at that tourney, I went on an unofficial visit to RU with my father, my grandfather, and my godfather. Immediately, I knew I wanted to go to there. The family atmosphere, along with the basketball tradition, engulfed me right away. Most importantly, CVS reminded me so much of my mother. Her presence was so regal and genuine; I was in awe of her but also felt very comfortable around her, and before we even spoke about basketball, she offered me a guarantee to get a degree. She was excited that I could potentially be one of the first doctors under her tutelage, and her enthusiasm to become the first became mine. I made my verbal commitment to Rutgers on August 29th, 2005. There's that 29 again!

"CHAMPIONS AREN'T MADE IN THE GYM. CHAMPIONS ARE MADE FROM SOMETHING THEY HAVE DEEP INSIDE THEM – A DESIRE, A DREAM, A VISION."

—MUHAMMAD ALI

# 14

## THE RU FAB FIVE:
### CONFIDENCE IS THE BIGGEST QUALITY YOU MUST POSSESS AS A STUDENT-ATHLETE.

No one else can live your life but you. So many people told me that I made the wrong decision when I chose to commit to Rutgers, and I thought otherwise. The naysayers said I wouldn't play because there were too many guards already there that were better than me. I didn't see it that way; I saw the bigger picture. I would be competing and playing alongside players who would elevate my skills. I knew I might not play right away, but I knew my time would come to prove my worth. Furthermore, I viewed myself as the most legitimate shooter coming into Rutgers at that time. Every team always needs a shooter, and I was confident I could fill that role. On a team with so many great players, everybody is talented, so you have to bring more than just your talent. My freshmen classmates and I understood that.

Judson Hall on Busch Campus at Rutgers University in Piscataway, NJ was the official home of our self-proclaimed, Fab

Five squad: Myia McCurdy, Epiphanny Prince, Rashidat Junaid, Delaquese (Dee Dee) Jernigan and me. Our five-member class was ranked first, nationwide by Women's Basketball Magazine in 2006. Additionally, we were the only school that year to land five Top 50 recruits with Stanford, USC, and UConn being the runner-ups. Scout.com made the national rankings: Epiphanny was ranked $10^{th}$; Dee Dee was $20^{th}$; Myia was $21^{st}$; I was $44^{th}$; and Rashidat was $45^{th}$. In retrospect, we really didn't care about the rankings; we were proud of that, but we still knew we needed to prove ourselves again. Frankly, your high school accomplishments mean nothing when you get to college; your slate gets wiped completely clean. Essentially, you earn the right to wear your school's name across your chest, and Coach Stringer made that very clear.

From the very beginning and also stemming from the nostalgia we felt during our official visit as high school seniors, we were very confident that we could come in and make a significant impact. Some may call it naïve, but we all knew we could bring some added value. We all went into our summer session extremely focused, ready to transition into college student-athletes. Our transition would not have happened without the leadership and guidance of the upperclassmen. That summer showed me why having upperclassmen was so important; they showed us the ropes and made us feel completely comfortable. That summer, we basically did everything together with the upperclassmen. Going to the movies, bowling, sitting in study hall, opening up bank accounts, learning the bus schedule, learning the campus, going on mall runs, eating out, working out, etc. were all done collectively. They really took us under their wings and took care of us, no matter what. Ironically, as much as we all did things together, the most exciting moments of that summer were when we played pickup against the upperclassmen. We would play, us 5, against the upperclassmen and whoever else was in the gym with us to build our chemistry as a freshmen unit and prove to ourselves that we rightfully belonged there. A lot of trash talking, sweat, and competitive fire ensued from those pick up games. Our self-proclaimed 'Fab Five' title also arose from those intense battles on the sweaty RAC floor. We held our own against the upperclassmen, winning some games and losing some games. We were competing with already established and impactful players in the Big East, and that was a remarkable feeling. I think we were a little full of ourselves and naïve after those games. We knew we could compete, but little did we know that the summer sessions were nothing in comparison to the actual, grueling season, three to four hour practices, or day-to-day operations of being a college student-athlete. We had no idea what it meant to be Scarlet Knights then. We learned over the course of that year what it really meant to be Scarlet Knights and what high expectations come from playing for a Hall of Fame coach.

**"I WANT TO COACH, CHALLENGE, AND ENCOURAGE. THERE IS A CERTAIN KIND OF RECEPTIVENESS THAT I NEED FROM A PLAYER."**

—C. VIVIAN STRINGER

# 15

## BE PREPARED TO MEET EXPECTATIONS. THE HIGHER YOU GO IN LEVEL, THE HIGHER YOUR EXPECTATIONS BECOME.

Not too many people have had the fortunate opportunity to be coached by a great coach, let alone a Hall of Famer. It is truly a gift and a curse to be on the receiving end of that coaching. On one hand, you are blessed to be coached by a Hall of Famer, but, on the other hand of the spectrum a lot of blood, sweat and tears are involved. Anyone who has ever had the opportunity to meet Coach C. Vivian Stringer knows that she has no grey areas. CVS, the friend, and CVS, the coach, are two totally different entities. Usually, this is the case with most college coaches who have consistent successful seasons. Off the court, the sweet, docile, nurturing, mother qualities permeate her interactions. You can have conversations with C. Vivian Stringer, the friend, about almost anything, from food to music to education to politics. She is extremely knowledgeable in so many things; I see her as a modern-day renaissance woman. That was the CVS who captivated me on my unofficial visit. On the other hand, CVS, the coach, is a fiery, passionate, determined, and extremely intense individual. That's the CVS I saw on the film *This is a Game, Ladies*, and that's who I wanted to be my coach. She is someone who brings out the best in others. Coach Stringer is an uplifter and an inspirer. Coach Stringer is in her element when she steps in the gym. She is always prepared to teach with her detailed lists of practice notes and is always ready to give you her undivided attention when a question is asked. She gives you her all, so she expects the same in return. She is one of the greatest teachers I've had the pleasure of studying under. If she's not teaching you about basketball, she's teaching you something about life. Her entire demeanor changes when she steps on the court. You can feel it in her presence and aura when she walks into the gym; you can see it in her eyes as she instructs drills; and you can hear it in her voice when she demands absolute excellence. Basketball consumes her entire being, and anyone who steps into that gym to watch one of her practices notices it immediately. She challenges you to become the very best version of yourself in all aspects.

From my experience, that best version of yourself does not come out unless you are well conditioned, mentally and physically. Every player who has ever played for CVS also knows that no player can attend the first day of practice unless she can pass her three-fold test proving her basic conditioning. It's a rite of passage for each and every player to be worthy enough to get onto her court to practice. You pass the test, and you're ready to participate in her grueling, 3-4 hour, non-stop intense practices. The test is a compilation of on and off-the-court conditioning. Each part of the test is completed, one after the other, with small, fifteen-minute breaks in between. Part 1 is a timed mile, 4 laps around a standard track. Guards had to complete a mile in 6:10 and posts in 6:30. Part 2 is completing five timed 55 meter sprints (55s 2x, 54s, 53s, and 52s, respectively). These are not the aggressive defense tactics she is known for but the double suicides that also have the same name. Suicides consist of running to multiple progressively distant lines on the court within a set time: free throw line, half court line, opposite free throw line, and opposite baseline. Now, multiply that by two, and you have a 55. Part 3 is completing the dreaded ladders. Ladders are a variation of 17's which involve running from sideline to sideline or, as our strength and conditioning coach called them, 'up and backs' in timed sets. The first set is one up and back, or 2 touches in 7 seconds; the second set is 4 touches in 15 seconds; the third set is 8 touches in 30s; the fourth set is 12 touches in 45s; and the fifth set is 16 touches in 60 seconds. Then, go all the way back down the ladder to complete the drill. Each part must be completed in the required times in order to pass. Fail any one part and you have to take it again. Fail the first part and you still have to complete the other parts. Pass or fail that day, you're taking the entire test.

Yes, we physically prepare all summer and the beginning of fall to complete this test, but, despite all the physical training, this test is 90% mental. It really develops and strengthens your mental fortitude; it pushes you far beyond the limits you thought you had. If your mind is weak, your physical capabilities are compromised. The strength of your mind holds more weight than your physical abilities any day. CVS's required conditioning test proved our ability to push through mental and physical fatigue to meet our goal of being able to practice. As much as you think you might die while doing this test, no one under CVS' watch has ever actually died. CVS clearly understood the mental benefits of physical conditioning, but at the beginning of my freshman year, she was extremely frustrated and disappointed.

In 2006, probably for the first time in her coaching career, CVS modified her practice rule because, on the date of the conditioning test, only 4 out of 10 players passed the test and none were freshman. Personally, I failed the test three times before I passed. Needless to say, as a collective, we were not physically or mentally conditioned in the beginning, and we started the season, 2-4 that year. I cannot speak for all of my teammates, but I'm sure they will agree with me when I say that it was never our intention to contribute to CVS feeling like she was coaching a team that she felt was the worst in her career. She vehemently expressed in our initial practices that we were the worst and most stubborn group of individuals she ever had the displeasure of coaching. In the beginning, we could tell she was disgusted with us, especially us freshmen. Her facial expressions constantly displayed feelings of distaste. She always told us we lacked discipline. We lacked timing. We lacked patience. We lacked mental toughness. We lacked conditioning. We pretty much lacked everything that she expected. We were by no means anywhere up to par with her expectations, and her expectations were high.

Transitioning from high school into college is not a smooth transition by any measure. In high school, you can get away with a lot of small things because your talent compensates for everything else. In college, the players you compete against are faster, stronger, and a lot smarter. I remember, in the aftermath of many of our first official practices, my freshmen classmates and I would have discussions in Judson Hall as to which one of us pissed CVS off the most that day. We would discuss how much we messed up or how much we got screamed at. It was a total disaster in the beginning. We were not trying to start the season 2-4; we did not intentionally try to get blown out by Duke by 40 points at our first home game. I vividly remember the 40 point loss to Duke. I started that game and played like a freshman, very timid, making turnovers, not playing well at all.

We got embarrassed so badly that CVS called a timeout towards the end of the game to make a statement to us. In the beginning of that timeout, she told us all to look up at the stands and watch our fans leaving. She vehemently said, "Look at how they are turning their backs on you because of the horrible performance we displayed." And then she said, "I don't blame them." That hurt. After the game, we heard a mouthful from our assistant coach Jolette Law; she scouted that Duke game and was livid. We never wanted to get our locker room privileges revoked. That was not the plan. We were trying to come in and uphold a legacy and a tradition that we thought we knew how to uphold. We were trying to do it our way, and that didn't work. We did not really understand the work it took, we only had hints of that knowledge. It took the older, more seasoned alums coming back to tell us about our lack of effort and pride, for us to buckle down and see the bright light at the end of the tunnel.

" WHEN TIMES ARE DOWN, KEEP BELIEVING, KEEP WORKING HARD, AND THINGS WILL PICK UP. "

~HARRY KANE

# 16

## LEARN FROM THOSE WHO COME BEFORE YOU.

"*I'm supposed to be the franchise player, and we're in here talking about practice. I mean, listen, we're talking about practice. Not a game. Not a game. Not a game. We're talking about practice.*" Remember that famous rant by Allen Iverson? His sentiment does not apply to the collegiate level; practice is taken very seriously. I will even go as far as to say that practices at Rutgers were harder than the actual games. We competed against ourselves and against the practice players, usually guys who play recreational basketball on campus. I saw no problem playing against guys because I've played against boys my entire life. Some people claim that it's not safe, and it takes away opportunities from women to fill those positions, but I disagree. That's another topic to discuss, but, in my experience, the guys were tremendous and challenged me everyday.

For those not aware, during the Christmas break, colleges and universities have no limitations on how much they can practice because school is not in session. These sessions, for most student-athletes, are known as 2-a-days. Many coaches see this as a critical time to teach and develop their student athletes a little more before the second half of the season starts. One particular 2-a-day was very crucial in helping to spark a sense of pride in all of us. It just so happened that on this particular 2-a-day we received visits from alums who basically schooled us on everything CVS had been telling us to do for months. The old heads: Cappie Pondexter, Tammy Sutton-Brown, Michelle Campbell, Mauri Horton, Nikki Jett, and our coach at the time, Chelsea Newton all showed us how much detail mattered and other lessons CVS was trying to get into our stubborn heads. The old heads made sure we heeded their advice by separating us into groups to pay closer attention to them.

Guards paired up with guards and posts with the posts. My alum guard, Mauri Horton showed me why I couldn't effectively get open from defenders. I was not paying attention to being effective in my movements; I was not sitting and sealing. I was not exploding to the ball with my target hand. I was being lazy. She showed me I was not upholding the tradition, I was settling for being average and not elite. Cappie instructed Piph and Dee Dee. Tammy and Michelle instructed Rah and Myia. We all got schooled by our alumni counterparts. That day's practice was a hands-on, CVS basketball education session. When it comes to upholding a tradition, it is very important to listen to those who have become before you because they act as guides to help you get through the similar situations you will encounter. The alums made me realize my selfishness and that the game was bigger than me. They made me realize my mistakes, but most importantly they showed me how to correct them. They showed me what being a Scarlet Knight was all about! They showed me that playing the right way went above talent; it included tremendous effort, consistency, pride, and attention to detail.

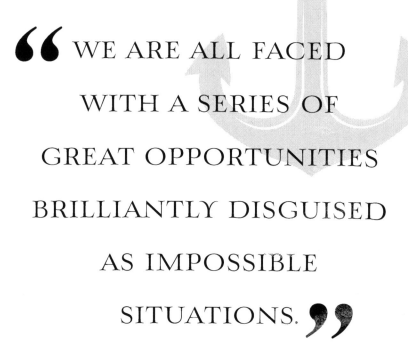

" WE ARE ALL FACED
WITH A SERIES OF
GREAT OPPORTUNITIES
BRILLIANTLY DISGUISED
AS IMPOSSIBLE
SITUATIONS. "

—CHARLES R. SWINDOLL

# 17

NCAA TOURNAMENT 2007:
TEAMWORK MAKES THE DREAM WORK.
"JUST BE A BETTER TEAM ON THAT DAY."

—C. VIVIAN STRINGER

Upholding a legacy and tradition is not an easy thing to do. As the season progresses, you understand that nothing is given to you just because your name is on it. Rather, everything is earned. I truly believe that the alums, having already gone through the same experiences, felt responsible to give their assistance and instruction so that we wouldn't taint their legacy. The year prior to us arriving on campus, Rutgers made it to the Elite Eight and expected nothing less from us. They wanted us to buy into the system. We knew what we were capable of but needed to completely buy in. Before the break, three freshmen, myself included, helped beat the very talented Armintie Price and the Ole Miss team in 3 overtimes when our upperclassmen fouled out. That game revealed our potential.

That on-court education by the alums spurred a sense of pride and confidence inside of us. We bought in; we, as freshmen, shifted our frame of thinking and thought in terms of TEAM. We bought into the system of intangibles and detail, the system of pride mixed with skill, consistency, and focus. We got better, and it began to translate to the games more. The freshmen began to show up in big ways. In one game following our Christmas break, my roommate at the time, Myia McCurdy, led the resurgence of CVS's most feared defense, the 55, and helped us bring down #22 ranked Pittsburgh at the RAC. Most notably, Epiphanny Prince and Myia McCurdy played significant minutes and made key plays, enabling us to upset UConn and capture RU's first ever Big East Championship. Nobody expected us to win that game, or even make it to that game, so it's nice to brag about beating UConn on their own floor once in a while. Our shift in mindset combined with the struggles early in the season toughened us up and propelled us into success during the 2007 NCAA Tournament.

The 2007 NCAA Tournament for us was mystical and magical. Finding out on Selection Monday that we were in the same bracket as Duke, the #1 overall seed, the #1 seed in that bracket, and the same team that blew us out by 40 points on our home court, was initially tough, but eventually blossomed into a blessing in disguise. The motto for season #3, or the NCAA tournament, was to just be a better team on that day. The teams we had to get past en route to the Final Four, with the exception of East Carolina, were teams we faced or were supposed to have faced earlier that season. Duke, Michigan State, and Arizona State were all in our bracket and were all in our way.

After we breezed by our first opponent, East Carolina, we beat Michigan State on their home floor as the higher seed. I played significant minutes and contributed a few timely shots that game, so I was on cloud nine. The following week, we went on to compete in Greensboro, NC for the Regional Tournament. We would get what we asked for, a chance to redeem ourselves against Duke after they embarrassed us earlier in the year. As the fourth seed, we stunned top-seeded Duke in spectacular fashion. With only seconds left in the game, my classmate, Epiphanny Prince, stole the ball and went coast-to-coast for the go-ahead basket to lift us to a 53-52 victory over Duke. Even more stunning, Lindsey Harding, the ACC Player of the Year that year, had an opportunity to win the game for the Blue Devils after she got fouled by Myia with one-tenth of a second left, but, somehow, she missed both free throws. We slayed the dragon; we got our redemption, and it felt really good. Only fate would have us meet a team that we were supposed to play earlier that season to get to the Final Four. Earlier that season, at the Paradise Jam in the US Virgin Islands, we were supposed to play the Arizona State Sun Devils, but the game was canceled when one of the brothers of an Arizona State forward died unexpectedly of an enlarged heart. This game was our rematch, and we bulldozed past them. We scratched, clawed, and willed our way into the Final Four. We got CVS back to the Final Four, a notion that we could have never even fathomed if you told us that at the beginning of the season!

66 THE STRENGTH OF
THE TEAM IS EACH
INDIVIDUAL MEMBER.
THE STRENGTH OF EACH
MEMBER IS THE TEAM. 99

—PHIL JACKSON

# 18

# FINAL FOUR 2007:
## UNDERSTAND THAT THE TEAM'S GOAL IS BIGGER THAN YOUR PERSONAL GOALS. YOU ARE ONLY AS STRONG AS YOUR WEAKEST LINK.

Every high school student-athlete dreams of unlimited gear heading to play collegiate ball. I remember my brother coming home on his short breaks from Villanova with gear for the family. That's what I wanted, and that's exactly what I received, especially during the Final Four. Imagine walking into a hotel banquet room full of Nike gear, as if you stepped into the Nike Factory store. My dream was no longer a dream: I made it to the Final Four. I believe it is every kid's dream to participate in March Madness. The first day we arrived in Cleveland, we walked into a room dazzled with RU colors and filled with bags full of gear with our names on it. We went from getting our practice gear and locker room privileges revoked to standing in a banquet room with our school colors everywhere with Final Four gear lying at our feet.

At that moment, I felt overwhelmed with emotion and knew that this team I was a part of helped me experience the most transformative season I'd ever had as a basketball player. They helped me reach the goal I dreamed of as a little girl, being a part of a team that displayed excellence, just like the Yankees. This team showed me that anything is possible with hard work and dedication. This team taught all the intangible qualities that one must possess to be successful in this life: leadership, resilience, selflessness, commitment, composure, and fight. I experienced the lowest of the lows and the highest of the highs, all in one year. I experienced a 180 degree turnaround and realized how a team operated. We became a complete team, and everything was done for the progression of the team. Everyone understood their role and excelled in them. We all accepted our strengths and weaknesses. Our chemistry with one another was phenomenal. As a collective, we masked the weaknesses!

In the National Semi-Final against LSU we shot lights out, but what was more impressive was that we played some of the best defense a team under C. Vivian Stringer had ever played. We held LSU to its lowest point total that season. Our stifling defense led us to a 59-35 victory over the very talented Sylvia Fowles and the LSU Tigers. I hit the last shot of that game off of a right-wing flare screen, running the spread offense. That night was unbelievable and one I will never forget.

Now, the National Championship is a hard game to get to. We advanced to the National Championship against the Tennessee Volunteers. I couldn't believe we made it there. We really made it to the last game that everyone wants to get to. To my dismay, we were not the better team on that day. We did not play well the night of the National Championship. We might've hit all of our shots two nights before against LSU. We couldn't buy a basket and we got hammered on the boards. We gave up

22 offensive rebounds. We failed to block out. We played hard but not smart. We abandoned what got us there in the first place. We did not win it all, and it hurt. I was overwhelmed with regret. If I only played a little bit better we could've won. If we only boxed out a little better, we could've won. We turned up the urgency too late in the game. We blew it on the biggest stage possible. I was devastated and heartbroken. I failed to get CVS the National Championship she deserved. We failed after coming so close.

**" DO NOT LET THE ROLES YOU PLAY IN LIFE MAKE YOU FORGET WHO YOU ARE. "**

—ROY T. BENNETT

# 19

## ALWAYS STAND UP FOR WHAT YOU BELIEVE IN, ESPECIALLY WHEN IT'S NOT THE POPULAR THING TO DO.

I felt devastated after losing the national championship. One of the reasons I came to RU was to compete for a National Championship, but never in my wildest dreams did I think it would come in my first year. We had an opportunity to achieve a feat no other team under C. Vivian Stringer had accomplished, and we failed. I failed. We were supposed to win that championship for Coach, and not doing that ate me up on the inside. It still does to this day. I didn't even eat after the game that night. All I could do was think about the loss; I could only think about what I could've done better. I was ashamed that we let something like that slip away. Eventually the love and support of my family, my teammates, our fans, and my friends helped me snap out of my low spirit. They helped me realize how much more we accomplished, despite losing in the National Final. We won 17 out of our last 21 regular season games. We won the school's first and only Big

East Championship by slaying the mighty UConn and holding them to their lowest scoring output of that year. We played remarkable defense throughout the NCAA tournament. Ironically, the very thing that was our Achilles heel in the beginning of the season became our secret weapon in the end. We held East Carolina, Duke, Arizona State, and LSU to their lowest point totals of the year as well. I realized that we accomplished so much when I actually reflected. Life is much more than a game, as CVS would always say, and that statement was proved evident the next day.

On the morning of April 4th, 2007, while sitting in study hall, our Sports Information Director Stacey Brann shared Don Imus' comments with us. At that point in time I really had no idea who Imus was, I just knew he was some sort of radio personality. Initially, I thought it was a joke when our SID read over the transcript, but when I got a chance to read over the transcript myself I realized how egregious his statements were. Imus was extremely disrespectful in calling us "nappy headed hoes," as was his executive producer Bernard McGuirk in calling us "hard core hoes." For the first time in my life I was a part of an issue that was bigger than myself, an issue that women all over the world have to deal with on a regular basis: living in a world dominated by men and their ideologies. The words spewed from those men's mouths wreaked of misogyny, sexism and racism all in one phrase. Until that day, I had never seen CVS so furious. CVS was irate, a different anger I had never seen before. I was upset; the whole team was upset. Coach Stringer's anger matched all of our anger. Sitting in her office during that spontaneous team meeting with our then Athletic Director, Bob Mulcahy, CVS made it very clear that we had to stand up for ourselves and make a statement. She made it clear that these men had no right attacking us. In no way did my team represent such a derogatory statement. If anything we represented the complete opposite.

From the very beginning, CVS made it clear to all of her players that once you put on that uniform you have a reputation to uphold other than your own. She made sure that we understood the significance of image and appearance because we represented her, the school, and our families both on and off our campus. Image and appearance were priorities. We were a team and, at all times, had to represent ourselves accordingly. While most collegiate teams were allowed to wear sweat suits and sneakers on travel days, we wore the same color mock neck shirts, khakis pants and acceptable black shoes. I and a few of my teammates despised this rule, but we did understand its purpose. CVS always made sure our hairstyles were neat and presentable; I failed to satisfy her standards a few times, and every time, with no hesitation, I heard an earful. At the end of the day, CVS had a standard, and everyone who has ever played for her knows this. So, from that anger we felt, we focused on what we could control and that was our response. We wanted to personally address the issue, to send a message to Imus that he picked the wrong team to make a "joke" about.

So on April 11, 2007, our team, along with CVS, held a press conference to voice our disdain and call out Don Imus and his executive producer. My teammates, Essence Carson and Heather Zurich, represented us that day. Every single word they uttered expressed the team's collective response: we would stand tall, confident, and proud regardless of those comments. Imus' opinion of us did not define who we were because we already knew who we were; no one could change that. That day, the world also knew who we were. As CVS called us, we were a Team of Destiny, a team that bounced back with resilience and fight. After our press conference, Imus did initiate a meeting and met with us face to face. We met at Governor Corzine's place that night. The regret he expressed went over my head, even though I sensed his good intentions. I really just wanted the meeting with him to teach him a lesson in accountability; you are responsible for the things you say. Our parents were able to attend the meeting as well, and the stories that I heard from my teammates' parents and loved ones, my mother, and my grandfather let me know that the feeling of love is the highest frequency a person can experience. The love that I felt in that room from my teammates and their parents was just what I needed to lift my spirit. I had a group of people willing to defend me no matter what. Imus started that scandal with hate, chauvinism, and bigotry, but we finished it with love, class, hope, and empowerment.

" THE BEAUTY IS
THAT, THROUGH
DISAPPOINTMENT, YOU
CAN GAIN CLARITY, AND
WITH CLARITY COMES
CONVICTION AND TRUE
ORIGINALITY. "

—CONAN O'BRIEN

# 20

## EXPECT DISAPPOINTMENT.
## WHEN ONE DOOR CLOSES,
## ANOTHER DOOR OPENS!

In life, disappointment is inevitable. I've been let down so many times, by myself and by other people, that I actually prepare myself to deal with it in most cases. Disappointment comes with the territory of having high expectations and standards. You must learn to be resilient when facing disappointment because a factor that measures the size of your success is how you handle and bounce back from disappointment. After a disappointing senior season by my personal standards, losing in the 1st Round of the NCAA, I was ready to embark on a new journey as a recent college graduate. At the time I had aspirations to attend medical school, but my intuition told me to put that on hold and see if my talents were good enough to play professionally. I hired an agent and thought I had a good chance to get drafted or at least invited to a draft camp. I assumed I was good enough because I thought I was a pretty decent WNBA Prospect. I had a decent agent who could vouch for me since I played under CVS. WNBA teams love players from Rutgers because we understand the game well, and I had a decent senior resume. I was the captain and leading scorer of an elite, Division I team, made an NCAA tournament appearance in the first round, made 2nd Team All Big East, and finished 2nd all-time in 3-point field goals made at Rutgers. I was anxious and nervous about the possibility of getting drafted because I already felt the heartbreak of not getting chosen in a similar situation earlier in my life.

In 2006, I watched my older brother make a case for himself with his remarkable body of work at Villanova and not get drafted. That hurt me a lot and I didn't want to live through that again! On the day of the 2010 WNBA Draft, I got a flurry of support from family and friends, text messages and phone calls wishing me good luck. By the end of the draft, my name was not called, and the same feeling of hurt that I experienced with my brother resurfaced. I cried that entire night feeling sorry for myself and asking why. I started to question and doubt myself after that. I thought I was good enough. Why did two of my teammates get drafted and not me? I knew I was a hard worker and that I gave it my all. I was devastated. I thought I had a decent senior season, leading the team in scoring that year, and actually making it to the tourney with a team that was relatively young & inconsistent. I was hurt and felt it for some time, but, as always, with the support of my close family and friends, I got over my heartbreak and just prepared myself for the next move. My mom even offered an alternative perspective, she told me maybe everybody still thought I was going straight to Medical School, and that's why I didn't get picked. I'm sure that had nothing to do with it because I hired an agent well before the draft, but, as usual, my mom came to help me see a different angle. She made me see that it wasn't the end of the world, and that it was actually a part of a blessing that I did not initially see.

Disappointment is a part of life, but it is up to us to either let that disappointment consume us or to take it on the chin and move past it. Let's just say I moved past it, and two new opportunities presented themselves. A month after graduation, I received two important calls; one was from my agent, and one was from a very good friend. The former call was an offer to play in Belgium, which I gratefully accepted. The latter call was the opportunity to represent the Bronx in the Empire State Games in Buffalo, NY that summer. I couldn't pass up on that offer and said yes. I guess the universe had something else in store for me. Ultimately, I helped represent the Bronx, and our team competed well enough to capture the coveted gold medal. It was the first medal the Bronx Women's team had won in 19 years! Not getting drafted hurt, but, without that hurt, I would have never been able to win a gold medal, build new friendships, and play basketball in the beautiful, small city of Namur!

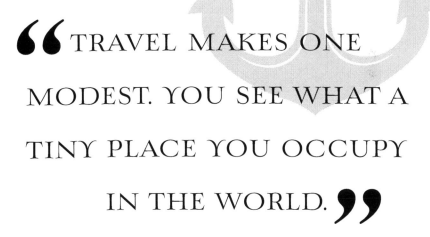

**"TRAVEL MAKES ONE MODEST. YOU SEE WHAT A TINY PLACE YOU OCCUPY IN THE WORLD."**

—GUSTAVE FLAUBERT

# 21

## LEARN ABOUT CULTURES OTHER THAN YOUR OWN. TRAVEL & EXPERIENCE THE WORLD.

Whether you travel for personal or professional reasons, traveling is a must for every person! Your perspective on life expands when you experience cultures other than your own. I know people all over the world, now, because of basketball. Basketball has allowed me to visit many beautiful places. I am forever grateful for the experience, and if you ever have the opportunity to go abroad, do it.

My first and only year as a professional basketball player was spent with Dexia Namur Capitale in Namur, Belgium, a city about an hour away from the capital of Brussels. It's a small city with a lot to offer a new college graduate. About three days after I arrived there, I spent seven straight hours exploring the massive Citadel, or Castle of Namur, that was located not too far from my apartment. Jean Francois, the owner/president of DNC, his wife, Virginie and children were so gracious to give me the grand tour. That's seven hours of steps, small bridges, a lot of winding roads, and more steps. Walking for hours was novel and a bit excessive for a New Yorker like me, but I enjoyed every moment of learning about the massive fortress, the point of meeting for the Sambre and Meuse rivers. In New York, the only river we have is the Hudson, and the Hudson does the Sambre and Meuse Rivers no justice. I was able to gaze at and stroll beside these rivers almost everyday. I definitely took that scenery for granted most days. It's a privilege to be able to immerse yourself in another country's culture, and I appreciated my time in Belgium.

Namur was a great place to be as a young adult coming straight out of college, and my hosts, the Davreuxs, and my American teammate, Katryna (Tree) Gaither, made my stay a lot more welcoming. I was fortunate to have an older, more experienced teammate like Tree because she helped me with everything. Shopping at the supermarket, driving me to practice because I didn't know how to drive a manual car, opening up a bank account, traveling to other nearby cities, and much more were all made possible with her guidance. My hosts, the Davreuxs, extended themselves more than they had to and gave me memories that I will remember for the rest of my life. Virginie taught me how to drive a stick shift car, which took a grueling three months, and she invited me to dinner every night (I had authentic Belgian meals almost every night). My favorite meal was a pasta dish with a dill cream sauce and salmon prepared two ways, smoked and baked. They even taught me how to prepare food straight from their garden, carrot soup and applesauce to be exact. I believe that was my first glimpse at the concept of farm to table, garden to table in that case; for them, it was their way of life to take items from the family garden, prepare them, and serve them at the family table. I was fascinated by this concept having grown up with only mediocre supermarkets most of my life. They took me to Disney World for the first time in my life; they took me bike riding most weekends; they took me to restaurants and so much more. Virginie helped me see that I shouldn't be cooped up in my room watching movies and shows all day, though that's the life you can be tempted to live overseas. She challenged me to enjoy the scenery, and I took advantage when I had the opportunity.

Traveling around the world gives you a chance to see that, despite differences in location, many of the same morals and principles you have are shared by other people in the world. The Davreux family showed me that, but most importantly Virginie was always at the forefront of those experiences. I had tremendous support from her, and her influence helped me adjust to life overseas more quickly. I became open to everything: the food, the culture, the language, and the city. My Namur family welcomed me with open arms. This is not the experience of every athlete playing overseas. I've heard many stories of teammates and organizations trying to sabotage players for no reason at all; I am grateful that that was not my experience. Although I was homesick, and it rained every day for the first few months I was there, I still had a remarkable time! My apartment, or my flat, as they call it, was spacious and walking distance from supermarkets, specialty shops, and walking and biking trails along the river. It was an extremely different vibe and atmosphere from the Bronx.

Every week I would visit the local farmer's market up the block from where I lived. I enjoyed rummaging through the local specialties: vegetables, jams, fruits, breads, pastries, herbs, etc! Picking out fresh ingredients to prepare at home made me feel like a real chef. Cooking became increasingly important to me due to my weekly farmer's market runs and my immersion into the Belgian food culture. In the beginning, I was lazy and didn't really cook for myself. I just ate sugary, Belgian versions of American cereal, made toasted sandwiches, and ate my local Namur favorites: durums, frites (fries) and waffles. Durums are basically variations of spit-roasted meat, lamb or beef, and in some cases, poultry, wrapped in a flatbread, served with various toppings like lettuce and sauce. Frites are exactly what they sound like; remove the letter 't', and you have fries. In my opinion, Belgian frites blow McDonald's french fries out of the water. To go further against the fast food holy grail, back when I indulged in fast food, I always preferred Burger King's fries over Mickey D's. Belgian fries reminded me of Burger King fries, but a better, upgraded version. Their huge, thick-cut wedges of potatoes are fried to a crisp on the outside, and chunks of warm starchy goodness fill the inside. My favorite dipping sauce was andalouse, which reminded me of ketchup and mayonnaise mixed together. Belgian waffles are nothing like their American counterparts you find in diners. The Belgian waffle is equivalent to a dessert. The yeasty, sweet, and fluffy waffle was my coveted sweet treat two days a week. Eating like that was not favorable for my profession. In fact, I became a little bit too heavy and was told by my team that I had to see the nutritionist.

That's when my perspective towards food shifted, and I knew I needed to change my habits. One of my top recommendations for aspiring professional players, especially if you are trying to save as much money as possible, is to learn to cook for yourself. You have greater control over what you put into your body when you are preparing the ingredients yourself. One of the greatest disservices athletes can do is consistently dump garbage into their bodies, in the form of junk food, fast food, colored manufactured drinks and so on. That was me eating whatever I wanted. And because I ate whatever I wanted, I struggled transitioning from high school to college and from college to the pro's. My eating habits were hindering my performance. I strongly encourage those pursuing a career in sports to implement a nutritional strategy into their overall development. Focusing on nutrition gives you a competitive edge over most other athletes. It can be the difference in you getting or not getting that next contract. Get in the kitchen, and learn to cook. You have more awareness of what is going into your body because you prepared it. Cooking is a skill you can use for the rest of your life. I not only reignited my love of cooking overseas, but I was able to live out my dream of traveling around the world. Playing overseas opened up the floodgates for me to travel the world and become immersed in cultures unknown to me. As a kid, I always traveled the world in the books I read. My imagination took me everywhere, and I always promised myself that I would get to do what I imagined about as a little girl. Playing professional basketball overseas helped me bring that promise to manifestation.

During my stint as a professional basketball player, I was able to travel extensively in Europe. Traveling immersed me in cultures and showed me how much this world has to offer. Everyday, I had the opportunity to explore, even though I did not speak the language. I was able to visit bigger cities in my country like Brussels, Liège, and Antwerp. I was also able to explore neighboring countries. Luxembourg, the Netherlands, and France were fun to visit. And because my team played in the Eurocup that year, I had the opportunity to travel as far as Venice, Italy and Minsk, Belarus.

Playing overseas helped me realize that I was no longer being coddled by my coaches, parents, and teachers. I was in the real world. Just like any job, being a professional basketball player overseas also had its pros and cons. I'm glad to say that I experienced a lot more pros than cons, but the cons still existed, and it would be a disservice to not share them. You are away from your loved ones for months at a time! I am a family person, and being away from home was taxing for me. You have to deal with major time differences and try to schedule days and times to speak to your loved ones. You may not get paid on time, or sometimes, teams may not even pay you at all. The amenities agreed upon in your contract may not always be there upon your arrival. Things like internet and cable may not be set up, and your dwelling place may be extremely different than what was agreed upon. I remember my contract stating I was supposed to get a washer and dryer in my flat; in reality, I only got a washer that was hooked up two weeks after my arrival, and, instead of a dryer, I got a drying rack. Most importantly, expect to be the leader. Much is expected of you, being an American on a foreign team. The referees never give you any calls and the other teams are consistently aggressive towards you. When you win, the team wins, but when you lose, it's your fault and the fault of the other Americans that may be on your team. The style of play and philosophies may be different from what you're used to as well. I clashed with my head coach about defensive and offensive concepts several times; our views were very different. The defensive principles that I learned at Rutgers were totally ignored, and that was a major conflict that I wrestled with my coach about. He basically went against every principle I understood to be true, which was extremely frustrating. You have to always take the good with the bad, I guess. Despite the cons, I am forever grateful that I had an older, more experienced, American teammate, who schooled me and that Jean Francois and his family welcomed me with open hearts and arms. Most importantly, traveling allowed me to realize that a person's destination is never a place, it is always a new way of seeing things. Going overseas allowed me to open up my perspective, and then, when I came back home, I began to find myself.

# Season III: Beyond
## Beyond I - The Transition

> "HOW STRANGE THAT THE NATURE OF LIFE IS CHANGE, YET THE NATURE OF HUMAN BEINGS IS TO RESIST CHANGE. AND HOW IRONIC THAT THE DIFFICULT TIMES WE FEAR MIGHT RUIN US ARE THE VERY ONES THAT CAN BREAK US OPEN AND HELP US BLOSSOM INTO WHO WE WERE MEANT TO BE."
>
> -ELIZABETH LESSER

**" STEP BACK IN PERSPECTIVE, OPEN YOUR HEART, AND WELCOME TRANSITION INTO A NEW PHASE OF LIFE. "**

—LINDA RAWSON

## 22

# TRANSITION FOR SUCCESS
# YOU CAN BECOME A PROFESSIONAL
# IN SOMETHING ELSE!
# FIND YOUR PATH AND THRIVE!

Being able to successfully transition to life after sports is the reality for many student athletes. Let's keep it real :less than one percent of collegiate student-athletes actually go pro, so entering the workforce is far more common. For me, transitioning into the real world was one of the hardest things I had to do as a former athlete. Frankly, I did not realize how much basketball ruled my life until after I stopped playing. I realized that basketball helped mold me into the person I am today; it has helped me build lifetime relationships; it has allowed me to travel the world and do so many interesting things. I had to come to terms with being a regular person after being a competitive athlete for most of my life. Once an athlete, always an athlete is a very true statement, but to transition into a life where sports is not the focal point of your day is difficult. Most of the time, an athlete goes from being an extremely active person, practicing everyday, games every week, traveling from city to city, gym to gym, to an almost sedentary lifestyle that doesn't rely on movement. True, some former student-athletes stay active but, in reality, most don't. The very movements that used to govern your habits, your routines, and your way of life become less influential. Training and practicing is not the norm anymore. Gyms and training rooms are no longer familiar. You adjust your life according to the profession you choose to pursue. These changes are not in tune with the way you've lived for most of your life. You move in a direction that is foreign in nature to you. That was me; after I retired, I got caught up in my everyday routine of working and spent less time taking care of myself.

Up until I retired from professional sports, I never had a real job in my life and realized, until that point in my life, playing basketball and going to school were my only jobs. I did not groom myself well for the transition because I did not adequately prepare for it. I strongly advise to all those trying to secure a successful future after sports to make it a priority to invest in every opportunity afforded to you as a student-athlete while you are still in school. Do not wait until you are a senior; seize every opportunity as soon as you set foot on campus. That is where I messed up, I did not take advantage of all my opportunities upon graduating from school. My senior year, I had opportunities to pursue other avenues besides choosing to play professionally overseas or going to medical school. I had an option to pursue a career in sports that I naively passed up on because, at that time, I had my mind made up. I put all my eggs in one basket and did not give myself an opportunity to explore other options. I will never forget the opportunity to this day. I got an email from one of my coaches forwarding a message from a publisher involved in the sports world. It was basically an invitation to a job in a sports exposure camp. It was the Diamond Sports Big Apple Career Camp. This camp provided student-athletes a rare opportunity to gain a competitive edge in the field and meet executives from ESPN, HBO Sports, the NY Mets, and more, at Yankee Stadium, Citi Field, Red Bull Arena, and Madison Square Garden. I did not act on what could have been a life-changing experience. I put all my eggs in one basket once I decided to go pro. Not once did thinking about my future beyond basketball cross my mind. That was a big mistake that I hope aspiring athletes will learn from.

Many of us think we will play forever and never stop to think about what we really want to do once we hang our laces up. I notice that some athletes, however, do set themselves up the right way to be successful after Father Time sneaks in. You see it more often now with WNBA, NBA, and NFL players gradually pursuing success after they are finished on the court or the field. Pennsylvania legend, Swin Cash, after playing 15 seasons in the WNBA, has transitioned into the front office, holding the title of Director of Franchise development for the New York Liberty, a job she was offered during her last season with them. She was already transitioning before she stopped playing. That is the goal, to solidify the next chapter before the sport phase is done. Chauncey Billups and Ryan Clark are also prime examples of professional athletes making a smooth transition into life after sports. Both of them set up their careers in broadcasting a few years before they retired. I did not set up my transition nearly as smoothly as they did.

Unfortunately, I did not prepare for the future, and I only played one year professionally. As much as I wanted to be a professional before I got out of school, when I became a professional, I was surprisingly not fond of the lifestyle. One of the things that is understood by all players who compete overseas is that you literally live out of your suitcase a majority of the year. I was not satisfied living out of my suitcase; I was not in tune with living that nomadic lifestyle. It made me uncomfortable living like that, being a homebody. You live away from your loved ones for months at a time, and that was difficult for me. If you're fortunate, you may get the opportunity to compete in the more competitive leagues in Europe within the EuroCup division or the EuroLeague. That means you get to travel a little more; you travel to countries further than your local region. If you've traveled enough within your own country you understand that traveling is exhausting. You consistently have to endure long bus rides and flights. Traveling week after week with several bags of luggage is grueling, and your attitude when traveling back is dictated by whether you win or lose. If you want to delve deeper, playing overseas for women is a little more taxing than it is for the men.

I believe women, professional basketball players have it a little harder than their male counterparts because many of them play all year round and barely get a break to recover and relax their bodies. If you play in the WNBA and play overseas, (basically the standard way to supplement your income), you make a very quick turnover from one season to the next. WNBA players have to supplement their income by going overseas because they make a fraction of what their male counterparts make. The average salary in the WNBA starts at around $50,000 and caps at $110,000. By comparison, the starting salary for the NBA is about $582,000. Can you imagine how you would feel if someone was doing the same job as you, but made 5x - 10x more than you just because of their gender? Can you imagine the amount of stress that is endured competing, traveling nonstop, and not really getting a legitimate break? This lifestyle did not represent what I wanted for myself, and although I could've stuck it out, I was tired. I was tired of all the aches and pains, the wear and tear on my body. I felt old at the age of 22 and did not want to live my life plagued with pain. I had two significant knee surgeries in college that consistently plagued me, and in my first year of professional competition I hurt my foot enough to force me out of a few games. My injuries played a major part in deterring me from continuing to play. I was mentally tired. Recovering from an injury takes extreme mental fortitude, and at that young age of 22, I naively made up my mind to stop.

More so than injuries, one of the biggest reasons I stopped playing basketball overseas was the fact that I could not live with the uncertainty of waiting. As a professional athlete, you must master being comfortable with being uncomfortable because that life entails so much uncertainty and waiting around. The uncertainty of waiting until your agent calls was difficult for me to handle, being a person who always needed a plan. I was a person who always needed to know how things would work out ahead of time. I was sitting in limbo, and that scared me. I knew other athletes who would, for months and even years at a time, wait for an opportunity from their agent. That was not how I operated, and that made me extremely uncomfortable. Just working out everyday and waiting for some good news from my agent made me feel extremely useless. The constant worry, the constant waiting, the constant wondering what my next move was bothered me tremendously. After my 1st professional season, I worried for 3 months before I decided to fire my agent and move on. Back then, living on my mother's couch for three months felt like an eternity, but, reflecting on it, I could've been a little more patient. I thought it would be easy for me to get a job after my decision, especially since I had a science degree. I thought I could easily get a job in a science company at a lab because of my resume. Job application after job application was denied; I had no experience and just a resume full of coursework that looked appealing.

I was a novice in the real world. I filled out so many applications to do work as a lab assistant, lab technician, and other miscellaneous jobs pertaining to science and medicine; all of them rejected me. Little did I know, the experience you gain before you enter your field of choice holds a lot of weight when it comes to pursuing work in the real world. In my opinion, getting your degree does not matter, what matters is how you make that degree work for you. If you do not diligently position yourself in college by attending workshops or seminars or completing internships before you stop playing, then it is really hard to transition to a successful career after sports. In retrospect, it's amusing that I ran away from uncertainty with the waiting game as a naïve 22 year old, only to stare it in the face again as a seasoned 27 year old.

As an entrepreneur I deal with uncertainty every single day. Not getting a steady paycheck every week, dealing with clients who don't pick up their phone when you've scheduled a meeting with them, and even business opportunities that I thought were fruitful turning out to be a waste of time are all situations dealing with uncertainty. Over time the uncertainty never changes, how you react to it does. I have become more comfortable with it, but anxiety around uncertainty is still very prevalent in my life. I say all of that to say this, I ran away from uncertainty to only realize that uncertainty was the very thing I should have owned in the first place. That uncertainty helped me find my way; it helped me figure out who I was. Life is uncertain, and we really don't know what life has in store for us until we go on our journey. I believe the journeys we go on help us to figure out what part in this life is actually certain for us! If we already knew our stories, then we'd live emotionless lives. The pure emotions that make us human, happiness, sorrow, anger, disappointment, struggle, and all the other things in between must be experienced to find out what we truly want. It is easier said than done, but learning to embrace uncertainty builds so much character. After I spent 3 months getting rejected by various medical and science companies, I decided to actually pursue something I loved instead of just finding another job. I followed my own advice and pursued an activity that piqued my interest. So many people get jobs that they cannot stand, so I wanted to get a job in something that I enjoyed.

That mentality spurred my relocation so that I could start fresh and surround myself with different scenery. I wanted to be learn more about food so I moved from NY to PA and enrolled at the Art Institute of Pittsburgh to start my culinary career, inspired by my travels around the world and my time in the kitchen at a young age. Cooking has always been natural for me. It has always been a passion of mine, but it was put on the back-burner because of basketball. Cooking has been a part of my life for as long as I've been aware of it. Before I decided to leave from my mother's side and tag along with my father to the basketball courts, I was at home in the kitchen with my mother. My mother and grandfather ignited my love of cooking from an early age. They offered me great variety in the foods that I ate. They showed me that food was the embodiment of bringing people together. My mother put together amazing meals every night. I can still remember the amazing dishes my mom made me as a kid: shepherd's pie, lemon garlic shrimp over parsley white rice, lima beans and oxtails, king crab legs with lemon butter. I was always excited to see what my mother prepared, day in and day out. My grandfather loved to put together big family feasts. As a child, TC would throw extravagant Kwanzaa parties for my entire family with mountains of food, from bouillabaisse and Moroccan lamb to fried chicken and collard greens. They planted the seeds for my love of food and love of cooking. Cooking was now my focus. It was my life after sports.

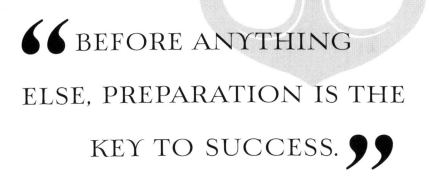

**"BEFORE ANYTHING ELSE, PREPARATION IS THE KEY TO SUCCESS."**

—ALEXANDER GRAHAM BELL

# 23

## IF YOU STAY READY, YOU WILL NEVER HAVE TO GET READY. ALWAYS STAY PREPARED!

If people are not asking me do I miss playing, they are asking me about my post sports career as a chef. My usual response, "It's fun if you like to work hard, if not, it's not for you," always raises a few eyebrows. In all honesty, you should be working hard at anything you are trying to do, one of the principles I try to live by everyday. I think people fish for the "It's really fun and enjoyable," cliché response, but I'd be telling you a partial lie if I didn't state otherwise. In no way am I saying that being a chef isn't fun; I'm just saying that hard work and pressure supersedes fun in the kitchen ninety percent of the time. Ever heard the saying, "If you can't take the heat, then stay out of the kitchen," well, a lot of people should heed that advice. I chose to pursue cooking as my next profession because it was my passion, not just because I wanted to try it out. I put cooking on the back burner because sports took the higher priority at the time. Cooking was introduced to me even before I learned anything about sports.

My former teammates can vouch for my genuine love of cooking. When I could I'd prepare meals for the team, and I'd watch cooking shows religiously when I didn't have homework or film to watch. I guess I knew back then that I wanted to be a chef; I just never really paid it any mind because basketball was my priority at the moment. I never even conceived of the notion of being a chef. Most people are the same way; we sometimes fail to think of using our most beloved gifts as a suitable job. I am here to say that you should move away from what society is telling you to do and move in the direction of what your heart tells you to do. Always follow your instincts and inner truths. What you may think is ordinary, may be extraordinary to someone else.

During my tenure as a member of the food industry, I was fortunate to work in very different professional cooking settings. My tenure included a chain restaurant, a high-end hotel, a luxury yacht club, and a farm-to-table restaurant. Just to offer some insight, being an actual chef in a professional establishment is totally different from being a celebrity chef. The celebrity chefs on television and the chefs in real life lead completely different lives. Cooking on TV is no comparison to the experience you would have in a restaurant kitchen, in a yacht kitchen, or even in a hotel kitchen. I highly advise that if you're reading this and have aspirations to start cooking for the simple fact that you want to become a reality TV star, then I'd like to say politely, "You should quit now." The Bobby Flay's and Rachael Ray's of the world do the easy work of cooking and talking about the food, but the real, meaningful work is found in the preparation of the food.

With anything that is successful, the foundation has to be of quality. Every good restaurant is founded on quality preparation habits. Truthfully, one of the most important aspects of being a chef is preparation. Being prepared is a basic requirement to operate a successful kitchen. Prep work makes or breaks a kitchen. Nothing is worse for a customer than ordering a delicious item on the menu and then being told by your waiter/waitress that it's not available. In some cases, it's acceptable to run out of something especially if it's popular, but to consistently not have an item is the misfortune of not having your station prepared and ready to go for service. Being prepared to work efficiently and effectively is the number one priority. Your life is surrounded by a set number of tasks you must complete and get done. In a way prep work and, in turn, prep lists govern your life. These lists help you remain diligently focused on the work you have to get done. The lists help you stay on track. Real life chefs use these lists to bust out the dirty work. Chefs work extremely hard and their days are long, grueling, and tiring.

One of my first days working at a hotel consisted of breaking down boxes of fruit for 7 hours to prepare fruit platters for a huge banquet event that was going on that evening. To give you a visual, I broke down the equivalent of Sam's Club wholesale boxes of pineapples, cantaloupes, and honeydew melons for 7 hours. Needless to say, it wasn't as easy as watching Anne Burrell divulging restaurant secrets like I had watched so innocently in my dorm room while in college. By the end of that first shift, I had blisters all over my hand. Oh and should I mention the burns that you experience! It should be a requirement for human resources to mention the amount of burns you get working in kitchens before you get hired. Nevertheless, during my time in kitchens, I endured long grueling hours, hot stoves, hot pan handles, hot ovens, and completing long prep lists, day in and day out. Completing tasks in the kitchen is laborious work and takes a bit of strength, both physical and mental. On delivery days, when your meats and produce arrive, lifting and breaking down heavy boxes is normal. Cleaning dirty fryers of sludge and extremely hot oil and then disposing that old, hot oil without severely burning yourself is normal. Pressure from your executive chef to have a successful shift of service is normal. Stress to have all your items prepared before service or an event starts is normal. If you don't like the pressure of meeting deadlines, then don't even think about becoming a chef. As I grew in the culinary world, my prep lists became a little more detailed, and making prep lists helped me understand why my mother made me write down my goals for so many years before. Writing your goals down makes you focus on them that much more; that way you actually start crossing them off. Those goals turn into crossed out tasks, and eventually, new lists are established. New lists and new goals, then, are ready to become old lists and old goals. Write down your goals, that way you see them everyday. The more you see them, the more likely you are to act on them. As you understand by now, I'm all about action.

**"** A MAN WHO STANDS
FOR NOTHING WILL FALL
FOR ANYTHING. **"**

—MALCOLM X

# 24

## DETERMINE & KNOW YOUR WORTH, OR SOMEONE ELSE WILL DETERMINE IT FOR YOU.

The vision you have for yourself may not be the same vision other people have for you. That is okay, but just understand, at the end of the day, other people don't live your life. You live your life the way you see fit. It was made evident to me that my vision was not the same as my superior's when I was I working as a prep/garde manger chef at a prestigious yacht club. I came into that job with an extremely open mind and a willingness to work hard to add value to that kitchen, but I quickly realized, a few months in, that I was not being valued as much as I wanted to be. My boss was trying to limit my growth by limiting the jobs I could perform; he did not feel like I was ready to tackle the hardest job in the kitchen, being a line cook. I successfully did my job as a garde manger chef, preparing salads, cold appetizers, and desserts for months on end. I wanted to tackle the next job at hand, which was being a line cook. I felt I deserved an opportunity to at least train as a line cook, and I still didn't get even that. When you're an ambitious person, you consistently pursue self-improvement, and with improvement comes more responsibility. I was ready for the greater responsibility, but my boss did not share that sentiment. We were on totally different frequencies, but over time, I learned that as you maneuver through life you will encounter many people who will try to put a label on you. They will try to limit your abilities, confine your potential, and define who you are.

My boss only wanted me to fulfill positions that needed to be filled for the Yacht club's benefit and not mine; I felt like I was just being used. I was learning, but not at the pace I felt I deserved. In hindsight, it's no surprise that my time at that establishment was the shortest tenure of any professional cooking job I've had. I felt that my boss was too restrictive and wanted me to do things at his pace. I was always being micromanaged and undervalued. He refused to help me grow and develop as a culinary professional. That was a sign for me to leave. In life, we all have choices, and at that point in my early career, I knew that my boss did not have my best interests at heart, whether it was intentional or not. It is crucial how you know your worth, set goals, and surround yourself with energy that reinforces your worth. You always have the option to put yourself in the best possible position, no matter what. Just always make sure you have a plan. Before I finally decided to quit my job, I was already actively seeking other employment opportunities. Leaving that job lessened my stress and put me in the right frame of mind to further my career in the culinary arts. I knew what I needed to do, just as you will when the time arises.

" THE MORE YOU TRUST YOUR INTUITION, THE MORE EMPOWERED YOU BECOME, THE STRONGER YOU BECOME, AND THE HAPPIER YOU BECOME. "

—GISELE BÜNDCHEN

## 25

## TRUST YOUR INSTINCTS AND TRUST YOUR BODY OF WORK.

Nearly every time that I have ignored my instinct or other feelings about a situation, it has turned out wrong. I'm sure the same can be said for you. Think about it, when we second guess ourselves and choose an option other than our initial thought, we usually regret it. That's why it's important to always trust what your gut is telling you. Your gut isn't some random feeling creating a sensation in your stomach; it's your soul screaming your truth at you, begging you to simply give in and be yourself. Give into it and trust it. I had to trust my gut feeling at one point in my culinary career to further my growth as a chef. I stated earlier that being able to accept criticism is a part of life and I stand by that statement. However, I also believe that criticism must be accepted only to a certain extent. You should not internalize critiques that you know are not true. One of the main criticisms I received from the boss that stunted my cooking growth was about my ability to cook on the line. Cooking on the line is one of the most stressful and exhilarating jobs a culinary professional can have. That boss constantly projected that I was not ready to be a dependable line cook and that my skills were lacking. I was told that I had to work my way up to line cook over the course of about 2-3 years. I didn't agree with that timeline and my gut was telling me that position was what I needed to expand my culinary skills. I knew that at my next job I wanted to prove to myself as an excellent line/sauté cook. I expressed to my boss that I felt ready to move up, but he failed to see the same vision. That's when I knew I had to leave. It was a messy break up, but leaving that toxic environment was very good for my spirit.

After weeks of searching for a new job through Craigslist, I found an opening for a pantry chef position, which would be cross-trained on sauté and grill, at a small farm-to-table restaurant. I went on the interview and got the job. I knew I could work my way up to line cook rather swiftly if I learned and improved everyday. I went from being the pantry chef/fry cook, serving appetizers, salads, and desserts, to the sauté/line cook, serving hot entrees/appetizers, in 6-8 months. I then went from being a line cook to being promoted to Sous Chef, the second person in charge of the kitchen, over the remaining 5 months I was there. At one point, I was running a 3 station line with 2 people, myself and my pantry chef, on Sunday nights. I went from being told I needed 2 to 3 more years of experience to advancing into a more skilled position in 6-8 months. I proved to myself that I could advance if I remained consistent and focused. A lot of people underestimate the importance of consistent effort. The consistent effort you give in any field of work is what separates the good from the exceptional. My consistent effort, day in and day out, little by little, moved me in the direction of my goal. I accomplished everything that I wanted to do in the professional cooking world; I proved to myself that I was the chef I knew I was meant to be.

# Season III: Beyond
## Beyond II - The Transformation

"THE MOST IMPORTANT JOURNEY YOU WILL TAKE IN YOUR LIFE WILL USUALLY BE THE ONE OF SELF-TRANSFORMATION. OFTEN, THIS IS THE SCARIEST BECAUSE IT REQUIRES THE GREATEST CHANGES IN YOUR LIFE."

—SHANNON L. ALDER

**I AM NO LONGER ACCEPTING THE THINGS I CAN NOT CHANGE. I AM CHANGING THE THINGS I CANNOT ACCEPT.**

—DR. ANGELA DAVIS

# 26

## YOU WILL ALWAYS HAVE THE ABILITY TO CHANGE YOUR SITUATION; DECIDE FIRST, AND THEN FOLLOW THROUGH WITH PRODUCTIVE ACTION.

Making the decision to work on yourself is no different from every decision you've ever made in your life. We all know when the need to change arises. It's an internal shift that happens, and it happens at different times for different people. Following my 26th birthday, I knew I desperately needed a change. I had slipped into an abyss during my new career as a culinary professional of which I was not proud. I did not realize I was in this state until I decided to take an honest look at myself. I was ashamed of myself; I had been an elite athlete at one point, and now I was everything I told myself I would never become. I was depressed, overweight, lethargic, and stagnant. I was going through the motions, feeling sorry for myself. So I decided to change that, and I chose to do better for myself.

That is what it takes, you being honest with yourself and facing all the things you do not like about yourself. It is hard to face your demons, but it is necessary if you want to grow. You cannot heal them if you are not willing to reveal them. Once I secured that new job at the farm to table restaurant, I did choose to invest in myself. I enrolled into the Institute of Integrative Nutrition to pursue my health transformation. My enrollment into this holistic health program changed my life and mindset. Through this program I began to see my body as an integrative entity. I began to understand that not just one thing would get me back to health but a compilation of things would. Our bodies are governed by so much more than just food. Our bodies are governed by our thoughts, our feelings, our relationships, our connections to nature, and so many other things we fail to realize. Immediately, I began to notice how everything began to change once I became more self-aware. I began to eat more nutritionally sound meals. I began to exercise again. I began to meditate. I began to show much more gratitude. The growth I experienced on my health journey propelled me onto the entrepreneurial path. I wanted to help people make breakthroughs with their own personal transformations, especially student-athletes. I wanted to make an impact and show people that if you consciously decide to choose to put yourself first, things will begin to happen for you.

**"CHANGE YOUR THOUGHTS, AND YOU CHANGE YOUR WORLD."**

—NORMAN VINCENT PEALE

# STRIVE TO DEVELOP A HEALTHY, POSITIVE MINDSET!

If you grow up like I did, you learn the concept of scarcity without even knowing it. I'd like you to think of scarcity as having limiting beliefs about certain concepts. This mindset is very narrow and reinforces the perception that you never have enough. You always think you need more: more money, more clothes, more food, more of everything. We are in such a constant pursuit of getting more that we really never pay attention to the things we already have. That was how I viewed the world. It never occurred to me that I thought in terms of scarcity for most of my life. I always thought I didn't have enough, and I needed more. I never really focused on what was at my disposal; I always concerned myself with always acquiring more. My mind flourished even in the perspective of scarcity regarding certain things in my life, despite all my accomplishments. I thought in terms of pessimism, in terms of doubt, in terms of worry, especially when it came to money. My lack of money was the biggest issue I faced. I always felt like I was losing money and not making enough to get ahead in life. I always thought money was this entity that I would never have; I really thought it was the root of all evil at one point. I never viewed it as anything else until I stumbled upon a lesson while taking a class to grow my business.

When I decided to invest in my entrepreneurial education, I took a business class that helped me understand the abundance mind frame. I learned that abundance was the concept I was looking for, and it was the antithesis of scarcity. Abundance was a word that I never associated with a mindset. I always thought about abundance as being associated with extravagant feasts like Thanksgiving and Kwanzaa. Abundance, I learned, is thinking in terms of optimism, seeing things from a more positive light. Thinking abundantly helped me realize that money was not evil and that it's actually an exchange of energy. If I put out abundant energy, I would receive the same back. Learning to think with great intention has allowed me to experience abundance. I finally found a word to describe this mindframe of thinking I grew to love. I was always abundant; I just never knew what it was called. Allow yourself to be open to new concepts and ideas. Your education is not limited to what you are comfortable with. You are very much in control of your growth as a person.

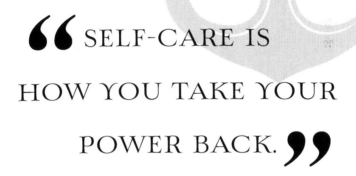

**" SELF-CARE IS HOW YOU TAKE YOUR POWER BACK. "**

– LALAH DELIA

## 28

# SELF-CARE IS ESSENTIAL! TAKE CARE OF YOURSELF 1ST, BEFORE YOU TAKE CARE OF EVERYONE ELSE.

After learning to think in an abundant mind frame, I was able to move more in the direction of self-care. Self-care is basically any activity that you do intentionally in order to take care of your mental, emotional, and physical health. In theory it's a simple concept, but it's something we often overlook. Good self-care is essential to improving one's mood and reducing anxiety. It's also key to having a good relationship with oneself. I learned the importance of this theory much later in life. I was very late to the game in learning how important mental and emotional health were. I always took care of my physical health and didn't take my emotional and mental health as seriously. I know now that that was a mistake. It is extremely important to begin to invest in your mental and emotional health. Mental and emotional health are no longer taboo topics and are becoming more mainstream, so to pay attention to these things is not so hard. You have to come up with activities that work for you. It is a gradual process to learn how to take care of yourself and small strides should be made every single day. Your journey is only your own; take your time.

In my journey, I first began to adhere to a morning routine. This was my stepping-stone into self-care. Then I began to meditate more; I began to do yoga; I began to read more; I began to listen to my body more. I truly began to invest into myself. I truly began to investigate myself. We live in our bodies day to day, not knowing how remarkable they are. Most people are so stressed out that they forget about themselves; they cater to everyone else's needs. I realized that finding inner peace for myself everyday, whether it's five minutes or twenty minutes, has helped me stay sane and focused in this world full of distractions. It has helped me show more gratefulness. Invest and take care of yourself first.

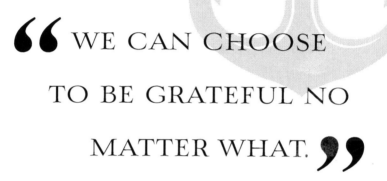

"WE CAN CHOOSE
TO BE GRATEFUL NO
MATTER WHAT."

—DIETER F. UCHTDORF

# 29

## GRATITUDE IS THE GREATEST GIFT
## YOU CAN OBTAIN.

When I was 9 years old, I almost lost my entire immediate family. I was involved in a scary car accident during a family car trip. My parents, my brothers and I were making a 11-hour car journey from the Bronx, NY all the way down to Columbia, South Carolina to visit my godmother. En route to the capital and maybe just under two hours from our destination, the tires on our car overheated and burst, sending the car off the road and tumbling into a ditch. I remember the screams, the shattering glass, clothes dispersing, and the car rolling over and over again until it came to a complete stop upside down. There was glass everywhere and I remember unstrapping myself from the passenger side seat upside down, falling directly onto the cracked front window glass. I crawled out of the broken passenger side window to find my older brother already outside of the car with his hand extended for me to grab. My younger brothers were still strapped into their car seats, yelling and screaming. My father somehow made it out of his driver seat unscathed and was able to get them unstrapped and out of the car. My mother, however, was the most affected by this accident. About an hour before we got on the road, my mother and I switched seat positions in the car. I moved from the back seat with my older brother to the passenger seat in the front. He sat on the middle seat with my younger brothers and my mom took the entire back seat for herself to lay down and get in a nap. Now, to put things in perspective, the two-seat stroller that was in the trunk came loose and fell on top of my mother, causing her lungs to collapse during that scary moment. Just an hour before the seat switch, my older brother and I were back there. That stroller could've have fallen on top of us, and we both could've ended up with potentially life-threatening injuries because of our small frames at the time. My mom inadvertently saved my life and my older brother's life by switching seats and taking on that big blow. The universe was not ready for our departure, and that is why, even to this day, I am grateful for everything that I have, everything I receive, and all the experiences I've had.

My life could have ended on that day. It took my self-reflection and exploration to realize how blessed I am. It took going through my entire journey to realize that gratitude is a powerful concept. Words are just as powerful as numbers in the frequencies they permeate. Your words are affirmations. You always hear the phrase, "put it out to the Universe", and it exists for a reason. Those words are hints given to you to see if you're paying attention. If you truly believe in something and talk about it often, you eventually make room for it to happen. Speak your truth into existence. I really delved into affirmations over a year ago, and they have done wonders for me. My mother blessed me with these specific affirmations: I am blessed; I am appreciative; I am grateful; and I am humble. I say these affirmations when I wake up every morning because

I know my time is limited. I know that life is uncertain. I know that time cannot be wasted. Showing gratitude helps you realize that time is the measuring stick. Time is the most important resource we have, and too many of us waste it on things that are so small. I realized that waking up every morning is the greatest gift you can be given.

Being grateful for the things you have in the present will ultimately lead you to allow room for receiving blessings in the future. Open your hands to give and everything will follow. Everything that has happened in my life has been made possible because of the support and love of others. I am grateful to be a student of so many amazing people. I am nothing without all of you. I smile because of you all! I am inspired because of you all. Groundwork 29 was made possible with the help of everyone I've encountered along my journey. To all of you I graciously say, "Thank you. You are all truly appreciated."

" WE NEED MORE LIGHT ABOUT EACH OTHER. LIGHT CREATES UNDERSTANDING, UNDERSTANDING CREATES LOVE, LOVE CREATES PATIENCE, AND PATIENCE CREATES UNITY. "

~ MALCOLM X

# Closing Contributions/Conclusion

What has been the groundwork for your success as a student-athlete and beyond?

### Allan Ray (Boston Celtics, 12-year pro overseas, Villanova Alum):

To be a successful athlete it takes a lot of sacrifice, discipline, and motivation. This is my foundation. This is what I pride myself on, and a lot of pro athletes do, as well. I was lucky enough to have a father that instilled these characteristics in me. When it comes to sacrifice it's self-explanatory. I had to make plenty of sacrifices when I was young. I knew that I wanted to be good and one day play in the NBA, so I used to always go out of my way to workout and better my game. I remember, before going out on weekends, I would drag my friends to the gym and workout. It would be, like, 10 at night, and right from the gym, we would go out. It's funny but it's true.

Working out and bettering my game was my priority. I knew that, by making that sacrifice, it would give me an edge on the competition. Having the discipline to do these things was also very important. For example, anyone can go to the gym and workout, but do you have the discipline to go hard every time or pay attention to the little details that will make you a better player? Disciplined athletes make it the furthest.

Last but not least, the motivation to keep working is important. The motivation has to come from within. Other people can motivate you to want to do something, but ultimately the work must come from you. I was completely motivated to become a better player. It got to a point where I could see all the good in being a great basketball player. One of the most motivating factors was being great at a game that I loved. I figured, why wouldn't I want to play basketball as a job when I got older? Everyone would love to work at a job that they love. Also, it would give me financial stability, which is what everyone wants in this world. It was an easy decision for me. So, basically, I would say find what motivates you, and don't stray too far away from it.

## Myia Johnson (McCurdy), WBB Assistant Coach at Penn State

My work ethic started at an early age. Every summer my parents sold candy, chips and slushees out of our house. All the neighborhood kids would stop by and we would completely sell out weekly. I would go downtown with my father to buy the slushee mix and then go home and pour the mix into the different size cups and place them into the freezer.

As I got older, my parents would allow me to answer the door, collect the money and serve the kids. I just loved this little job! The whole process of putting in work and getting paid just excited my soul. It taught me that hard work gets rewarded.

My parents always encouraged me to cut grass, rake leaves and to shovel snow for money so when the seasons changed, I would get excited because I knew the cash was about to roll in.

At a young age, I understood that if it was something I wanted it was attainable if I worked hard for it. This translated over to sports as well. My mother would always tell me, "While I'm not working, there's someone else in the world, working harder than me and they're trying to take my spot". This scared the mess out of me! I couldn't stand the thought of someone out working me or taking my spot. I never wanted that to happen so no matter what sport I played; I always made sure that I put in extra work.

My parents nor coaches never had to ask me if I was practicing outside of practice. I was internally motivated, self driven and hungry to be better everyday. As I got older my competitiveness grew stronger. I had developed life goals and I was determined to accomplish them one by one.

One of my life goals included: playing college basketball at the highest level! I knew that this goal would require sacrifices and lots of hard word. As a student athlete, I went through some of the most challenging periods in my life. However, I never gave up and I always visualized myself conquering the difficult moments.

If it wasn't for my parents instilling a work ethic in me at an early age, I wouldn't have achieved all the success that I've had in my life. My parents created the groundwork for my success and work ethic!

## Matee Ajavon (Atlanta Dream, 10 year WNBA veteran, RU Alum):

It took a lot of hard work and dedication to get where I am today. When you want to be successful, you have to have tunnel vision. That means cutting things and people off that may not be beneficial to the levels you're trying to reach. Learning to sacrifice takes discipline and great will, but it'll be well worth it.

**Essence Carson (WNBA Champion, Phoenix Mercury RU Alum):**

At an early age, I learned the importance of time management. Loving school, being involved in the arts since age 9, and being a participant in each sport season didn't allow for much free time. Nonetheless, I made time for the things I loved to do.

See, everyone always speaks of the amount of work it takes to become successful but fails to mention the balance of time. With anything in life, balance is needed, hence, yin and yang. Anything that is completely one-sided will eventually cause you to become overly stressed and lead to, what we call, burnout. Our balance allows us to seamlessly align our workflow in our lives and create a healthy environment for your success to live and thrive.

To sum up everything briefly, time management and balance have been the keys to my success. These two not-often-spoken-about attributes that continue to allow me to thrive are able to be taught and learned at a very young age - in my opinion they should be.

Name: Ray, Brittany
Study Hall: 8 Hours

**R**

# OFFICE OF ACADEMIC SUPPORT SERVICES FOR STUDENT-ATHLETES
## Fall 2006 Weekly Time Management Sheet – Week of October 29th

| Time | Sunday | Monday | Tuesday | Wednesday | Thursday | Friday | Saturday | Priority List (Cross off when completed) |
|---|---|---|---|---|---|---|---|---|
| 7:00-8:30 | | Practice 7:30 – 10:30 | Practice 6:00 – 9:00 | Practice 9:00 – 12:00 | Practice 7:30 – 10:50 | Practice 8:00 – 12:00 | | A. |
| 8:30-10:00 | | | | | | | | B. |
| 10:00-12:00 | | | Fundamentals of Speaking and Listening 9:50 – 12:50 Campbell – A2 | | Intro to Experiment 10:20 – 1:20 Beck – 052 | | Pre-Game Meal | C. |
| 12:00-1:00 | | Chemistry with Wana 2:00pm at RAC | Black Theology 1:40 – 3:00 Beck – 003 | Math with Kelley 1:00pm at RAC | Doug Up | | Arrive at RAC 12:50 | D. |
| 1:00-2:30 | | | | Chem 3:4, 24, 30 pm | Black Theology 1:40 – 3:00 Beck – 003 | Study Hall at RAC 1:30 – 3:30 Math with Kelley | RU vs Cincinnati 2PM | E. |
| 2:30-4:00 | | | | BE – 001 L-Retreat | 3:30- 4: 30 @ the RAC | | | F. |
| 4:00-6:30 | | | | | | | | G. |
| 6:30-7:00 | | Chemistry 5:15 – 6:10 Beck – Aud | Game vs Marquette At RAC 5:30 Game 7:00 | Calculus 5:15 – 6:10 B – 101 | | | | H. |
| 7:00-8:30 | | Chemistry 6:40 – 8:00 Beck – Aud | | Chemistry 6:40 – 8:00 Beck – Aud | | | | I. |
| 8:30-10:00 | | Calculus 8:10 – 9:30 LCB – 102 | | Calculus 8:10 – 9:30 LCB – 102 | | | | J. |
| Homework & Tests Due: | | | | | | | | K. |

## Rutgers University
## Women's Basketball Team Travel Schedule
## 2006 SPRING Semester

| OPPONENT | Home or Away | Date & Time Leaving | Date & Time of Match | Date & Time Returning | Class Periods Missed |
|---|---|---|---|---|---|
| GEORGETOWN | HOME | Tuesday, Jan. 16th 5:30 PM | Tuesday, Jan. 16th 7:30 PM | Tuesday Night | Tues., Jan. 16th 4:30 PM & Later |
| TEMPLE | Away | Tuesday, Jan. 23rd 1:00 PM | Wednesday, Jan. 24th 7:00 PM | Wednesday Night | Tues., Jan. 23rd 1:00 PM & Later |
| MARQUETTE | HOME | Tuesday, Jan. 30th 5:30 PM | Tuesday, Jan. 30th 7:30 | Tuesday Night | Tues., Jan. 30th 4:30 AM & Later |
| CONNECTICUT | Away | Monday, Feb. 5th 1:00 PM | Tuesday, Feb. 6th 8:00 PM | Tuesday Night | Mon., Feb. 5th 1:00 PM & Late Tues., Feb. 6th All Day |
| SYRACUSE | Away | Tuesday, Feb. 13th 1:00 PM | Wednesday, Feb. 14th 7:00 PM | Wednesday Night | Tues., Feb. 13th 1:00 PM & Later Wed., Feb. 14th All Day |
| VILLANOVA | Away | Friday, Feb. 16th 1:00 PM | Saturday, Feb. 17th 7:00 PM | Saturday Night | Fri., Feb. 16th 1:00 PM & Later |
| VILLANOVA | HOME | Tuesday, Feb. 15th 5:30 PM | Tuesday, Feb. 15th 7:30 PM | Tuesday Night | Tues., Feb. 14th 11:30 AM & Later |
| PROVIDENCE COLLEGE | HOME | Tuesday, Feb. 20th 5:30 PM | Tuesday, Feb. 20th 7:30 PM | Tuesday Night | Tues., Feb. 20th 5:30 PM & Later |
| NOTRE DAME | Away | Friday, Feb. 23rd 1:00 PM | Saturday, Feb 24th 12:00 PM | Saturday Night | Fri., Feb 23rd 1:00 PM & Later |
| CONNECTICUT | HOME | Monday, Feb. 26th 5:30 PM | Monday, Feb. 26th 7:00 PM | Monday Night | Mon., Feb. 26th 5:30 PM & Later |
| BIG EAST TOURNAMENT | Away | TBA | March | TBA | TBA |

Professor/Instructor's Name: _Kevin Castello_
(Please Print)

Professor/Instructor's Signature: _____

Date: _2/01/07_

Student-Athlete Signature: _____

Date: _____

Course: _____ Class Period: _____

*STUDENT'S COPY*

# DECEMBER 2006

## RUTGERS WOMEN'S BASKETBALL PRACTICE SCHEDULE

| Sunday | Monday | Tuesday | Wednesday | Thursday | Friday | Saturday |
|---|---|---|---|---|---|---|
| | | | | | **1** | **2** 8:00 AM - 11:00 AM Practice; Cager Kids Pizza Party |
| **3** 12:00 PM - 3:00 PM Practice | **4** 7:00 PM Jimmy V Classic RU vs Duke | **5** 9:00 AM - 12:00 PM Practice | **6** 8:00 AM - 11:00 AM Practice; Travel to DePaul | **7** 7:00 PM RU @ DePaul | **8** 11:00 AM - 1:00 PM Practice ?; 6:00 PM - 8:00 PM Practice | **9** 7:30 PM RU vs Princeton |
| **10** 12:00 PM - 3:00 PM Practice | **11** 7:30 AM - 10:30 AM Practice | **12** 7:30 PM RU vs Mississippi | **13** | **14** Happy B-Day Juleite; 7:30 AM - 10:30 AM Practice | **15** 9:00 AM - 1:00 PM Practice | **16** 8:00 PM RU vs Iowa; Ladies Knights Out Reception |
| **17** 12:00 PM - 3:00 PM Practice | **18** | **19** 7:30 AM - 10:30 AM Practice | **20** Day Off | **21** Read Day; 8:00 AM - 11:00 AM Practice | **22** Finals | **23** |
| **24** Winter Break | **25** Merry Christmas | **26** 8:00 PM - 10:00 PM Practice | **27** 11:00 AM - 2:00 PM Practice; 6:00 PM - 8:00 PM Practice | **28** 10:00 AM - 1:00 PM Practice; 4:00 PM - 6:00 PM Practice | **29** Day Off | **30** Winter Break |
| **31** 3:00 PM Men have a game; 4:00 PM - 7:00 PM Practice | | | Finals | | **29** 9:00 AM - 12:00 PM Practice; 12:30 PM Depart; 1:00 PM - 4:00 PM MBB Practice | **30** 1:00 PM - 4:00 PM MBB Practice; 2:00 PM RU @ ODU |

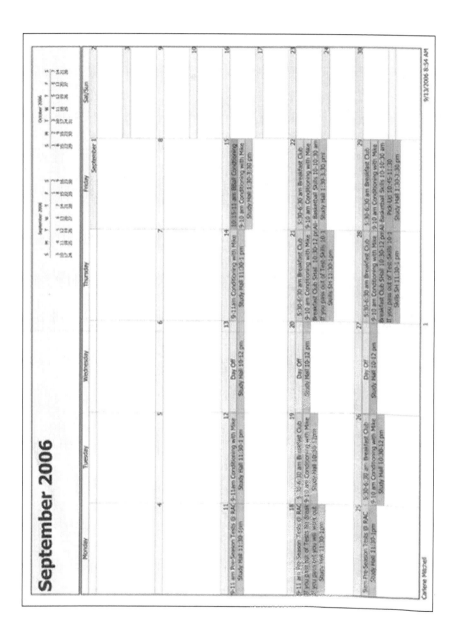

# September 2006

# JANUARY 2007

## RUTGERS WOMEN'S BASKETBALL PRACTICE SCHEDULE

| Sunday | Monday | Tuesday | Wednesday | Thursday | Friday | Saturday |
|---|---|---|---|---|---|---|
| | **1** 10:00 AM - 1:00 PM Practice; 7:00 PM - 4:00 PM MBB Practice? Depart | **2** 12:00 PM - 1:30 PM Shoot Around; 1:30 PM - 4:00 PM MBB Practice?; 2:00 PM - 3:00 PM Pre-Game Meal; RU @ St. John's | **3** 10:00 AM - 1:00 PM Practice; 4:00 PM - 6:00 PM Practice | **4** 10:00 AM - 1:00 PM Practice; 4:00 PM - 6:00 PM Practice | **5** 10:00 AM - 3:00 PM Practice; 4:00 PM - 6:00 PM Practice | **6** 7:00 AM - 8:00 AM Shoot Around; 8:00 AM Pre-Game Meal; 12:00 PM RU vs Pittsburgh; 2:00 PM Pizza Party |
| **7** 10:00 AM - 1:00 PM Practice; 4:00 PM - 6:00 PM Practice | **8** 10:00 AM - 1:00 PM Practice; 4:00 PM - 5:00 PM Practice | **9** 10:30 AM - 12:00 PM Shoot Around; 12:30 PM Pre-Game Meal; 7:00 PM RU vs USF | **10** 10:00 AM - 1:00 PM Practice; 4:00 PM - 6:30 PM Practice - The Barn? | **11** 10:00 AM - 1:00 PM Practice; 4:00 PM - 6:00 PM Practice | **12** 10:00 AM - 1:00 PM Practice; Depart for Seton Hall | **13** 2:00 PM RU @ Seton Hall |
| **14** 10:00 AM - 1:00 PM Practice; 4:00 PM - 6:00 PM Practice | **15** 10:00 AM - 1:00 PM Practice | **16** 10:30 AM - 12:00 PM Practice; 12:00 PM - 1:00 PM Pre-Game Meal; 7:30 PM RU vs Georgetown | **17** | **18** Happy B-Day Epiphanny; 7:30 AM - 10:30 AM Practice | **19** 8:00 AM - 12:00 PM Practice | **20** RU @ Louisville |
| **21** Travel Day | **22** ML King Day; 7:30 AM - 10:30 AM Practice | **23** First Day of Class; 9:00 AM - 12:00 PM Practice; Depart | **24** Day Off; 7:00 PM RU @ Temple | **25** 7:30 AM - 10:30 AM Practice | **26** 8:00 AM - 12:00 PM Practice | **27** 10:00 AM - 1:00 PM Practice |
| **28** Day Off; 9:00 AM - 10:30 AM Shoot Around; 1:00 PM Pre-Game Meal; 5:00 PM RU vs Michigan State; Ladies Knight Out | **29** 7:30 AM - 10:30 AM Practice | **30** 12:00 AM - 1:00 PM Pre-Game Meal; 10:30 AM - 12:00 PM Shoot Around; 7:30 PM RU vs Marquette | **31** Happy B-Day Kia; 9:00 AM - 12:00 PM Practice | | | |

### December '06

| S | M | T | W | T | F | S |
|---|---|---|---|---|---|---|
| | | | | | 1 | 2 |
| 3 | 4 | 5 | 6 | 7 | 8 | 9 |
| 10 | 11 | 12 | 13 | 14 | 15 | 16 |
| 17 | 18 | 19 | 20 | 21 | 22 | 23 |
| 24 | 25 | 26 | 27 | 28 | 29 | 30 |
| 31 | | | | | | |

### February '07

| S | M | T | W | T | F | S |
|---|---|---|---|---|---|---|
| | | | | 1 | 2 | 3 |
| 4 | 5 | 6 | 7 | 8 | 9 | 10 |
| 11 | 12 | 13 | 14 | 15 | 16 | 17 |
| 18 | 19 | 20 | 21 | 22 | 23 | 24 |
| 25 | 26 | 27 | 28 | | | |

## FEBRUARY 2007
### RUTGERS WOMEN'S BASKETBALL PRACTICE SCHEDULE

| Sunday | Monday | Tuesday | Wednesday | Thursday | Friday | Saturday |
|---|---|---|---|---|---|---|
| | | | | **1** 7:30 AM - 10:30 AM Practice | **2** 8:00 AM - 12:00 PM Practice | **3** 8:45 AM - 10:15 AM Shoot Around 10:30 AM - 11:30 AM Pre-Game Meal 2:00 PM RU vs Cincinnati |
| **4** 12:00 PM - 3:00 PM Practice | **5** Travel Day | **6** 8:00 PM RU @ Connecticut | **7** | **8** 7:30 AM - 10:30 AM Practice | **9** 8:00 AM - 12:00 PM Practice | **10** 10:00 AM - 1:00 PM Practice |
| **11** 8:00 AM - 9:30 AM Shoot Around 10:00 AM Pre-Game Meal 3:00 PM RU vs West Virginia | **12** | **13** 9:00 AM - 12:00 PM Practice Travel | **14** Day Off 7:00 PM RU @ Syracuse | **15** 7:30 AM - 10:30 AM Practice | **16** 8:00 AM - 12:00 PM Practice Travel | **17** RU @ Villanova |
| **18** | **19** Day Off 7:30 AM - 10:30 AM Practice | **20** 9:00 AM - 10:30 AM Shoot Around 11:00 AM - 12:00 PM Pre-Game Meal 2:30 PM RU vs Providence | **21** 9:00 AM - 12:00 PM Practice | **22** 7:30 AM - 10:30 AM Practice | **23** 8:00 AM - 12:00 PM Practice Travel | **24** Happy B-Day Chelsea RU @ Notre Dame |
| **25** 12:00 PM - 3:00 PM Practice | **26** 9:00 AM - 10:30 AM Shoot Around 11:30 AM - 12:00 PM Pre-Game Meal 7:00 PM RU vs Connecticut | **27** | **28** Day Off | | | |

# MARCH 2007
## RUTGERS WOMEN'S BASKETBALL PRACTICE SCHEDULE

| Sunday | Monday | Tuesday | Wednesday | Thursday | Friday | Saturday |
|---|---|---|---|---|---|---|
| | | | | 1 | 2 Travel | 3 Big East Tournament |
| 4 Big East Tournament | 5 Big East Tournament | 6 Big East Tournament Travel | 7 | 8 Happy B-Day Brittany | 9 | 10 |
| 11 | 12 Selection Monday | 13 Happy B-Day Michelle | 14 | 15 | 16 | 17 |
| 18 NCAA Tournament 1 & 2 Round | 19 NCAA Tournament 1 & 2 Round | 20 | 21 | 22 | 23 Happy B-Day Coach S. | 24 |
| 25 NCAA Tournament - Regionals | 26 NCAA Tournament - Regionals | 27 NCAA Tournament - Regionals | 28 | 29 | 30 | 31 |

# OFFICE OF ACADEMIC SUPPORT SERVICES
## FOR STUDENT-ATHLETES

Louis Brown Athletic Center
(732) 445-3826

Hale Center
(732) 445-5120

March 7, 2007

Dear Professor/Instructor:

     This is to verify that _____ is a member of the *Rutgers University Women's Basketball Team*. They were competing at the Big East Tournament that was held on March $2^{nd}$, $3^{rd}$, $4^{th}$, $5^{th}$, and $6^{th}$ in Storrs, CT. The team will be returning to campus on March $7^{th}$ as the <u>BIG EAST WOMEN'S BASKETBALL CHAMPIONS.</u>

     Our student-athletes understand they are responsible for all work and assignments while representing the University in an intercollegiate competition.

     If you have any further questions or concerns, please do not hesitate to contact me at 732-445-7865 or e-mail <u>mpeterson@scarletknights.com</u>.

     Thank you very much for your understanding in this matter.

Sincerely,

Mark Peterson
Athletic Academic Advisor

cc:     Vivian Stringer - Head Coach – Women's Basketball
         Kathleen J. Shank – Director Academic Support Services
                for Student-Athletes

*Official Team Photo of Dexia Namur Capitale Professional Basketball Team. (Namur, Belgium)*

*Opening Festivities for the New York State Empire Games. (Buffalo, NY)*

*Playing Point Guard for Dexia Namur Capitale. (Belgium)*

*Introduction of Dexia Namur Capitale Professional Basketball Team (Namur, Belgium)*

*Taking a picture with my team at Adidas Top Ten Camp. (Suwanee, GA)*

*New York State Empire Games Gold Medalists. (Buffalo, NY)*

*Kips Bay Boys and Girls Club Lady Mustangs 12 & under team. (Bronx, NY)*

*The morning after winning Rutger's First Big East Championship. (Storrs, CT)*

*Kips Bay Boys and Girls Club Lady Mustangs High School Division Team. (Bronx, NY)*

*NCAA Sweet Sixteen Game vs. Duke Blue Devils when E. Prince hit the tough game winning lay up to send us to the Elite Eight. (Greensboro, NC)*

*10 year high school reunion @ Aquinas High School. (Bronx, NY)*

*Enjoying a bite to eat overseas with my American teammate, Tree Gaither, her partner, Cynthia and my husband, Austin. (Brussels, Belgium)*

*Ms. Angeloni 3rd grade class @ Sacred Heart Elementary School (Bronx, NY)*

*My Beautiful Family: (t-b) My mother, Larnel, my father, Allan Jr., my older brother, Allan III, my middle brother, Kendrick and my youngest brother, Aaron.*

*My best friends, Whitney and Chanteé.*

*The RU Fab Five: (l-r) Dee Dee Jernigan, Epiphanny Prince, Rashidat Junaid, Me, & Myia McCurdy. (Piscataway, NJ)*

*Paradise Jam Opening Festivities with the team. (U.S. Virgin Islands)*

*The Davreux Family and I: (l-r) Violet, Me, Martin, Constance, Virginie, Jean-Francois and Clarisse. (Namur, Belgium)*

*The Fab Five at the Don Imus Press Conference. (Piscataway, NJ)*

*The Ray Clan: (l-r) Allan III, Me, Kendrick and Aaron.*

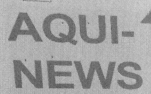
# AQUINAS: HOME OF NYS CHAMPIONS

*Back, from left: Ms. Socorro Santos-Winters '78 (coach), Naomi Solano, Dominique Pagan, Maria Turner, Alysia Saunders. Middle, from left: Jasmine Lassiter, Judith Ray, Shawn Pierce, Chantae Hallett. Front, from left: Idelissa Lloveres, Jennifer Powe, Dalila Garcia, Samantha Feliz.*

Hail to the Lady Bears who won a 62-52 victory over South Jefferson High School on Sunday, March 25, 2006 in Glens Falls to claim the New York State Federation Championship in the Class B Division of Girls Basketball - a first in the history of Aquinas High School!

Senior Alysia Saunders contributed 15 points and 12 rebounds. Judith Ray scored a memorable total of 32 points in the last game of her high school career. Next year Judith will be playing for Rutgers University. On 3/03/06 Judith was named Student Athlete of the Week by the New York Daily News.

The championship game was a true contest. Aquinas trailed 26-16 with four minutes left in the second quarter and South Jefferson took a 30-23 lead into halftime. But Aquinas used a 20-8 run through the third quarter to take control of the game. South Jefferson pulled to within 47-45 midway through the fourth, but Aquinas kept the lead, finishing 10 points ahead.

The New York State Federation of Secondary Schools Athletic Association is comprised of all four High School Athletic Associations in New York State. These members include the New York State Public High School Athletic Association, the Public School Athletic Association of New York City, the Catholic High School Athletic Association of New York City, and the Association of Independent Schools Athletic Association. Of the new head coach, [...] the NYS Championship Tournament, Ms. Socorro [...]

Santos-Winters was the sole woman. She inspired her team to the highest standards of achievement and sportsmanship. The Aquinas basketball varsity has both a victory and a role model they will always remember.

The road to the Federation Championship was filled with many intermediate victories in Aquinas' 27-3 season. The CHSAA championship was clinched in the final with Nardin Academy at St. John's University on March 18. Aquinas' cheering section was replete with students, parents, administration, faculty, and family of faculty - all waving the blue and gold supplied by the Santos family, who were present in full force.

Life since the championship game has held magical moments:
- Stepping off the bus after the 4-hour ride from Glens Falls to see Sr. Eileen Richard's sign in front of the school. AQUINAS HIGH SCHOOL BASKETBALL VARSITY: NEW YORK STATE CHAMPIONS.
- The tumultuous applause with the PA announcement by Sr. Catherine Rose on Monday morning, and the sporting of the Federation Championship shirts and individual medals by the team members throughout the day.
- The full school assembly in the circle Friday morning, with the Marching Band playing, and the Champions up front and center.
- Sr. Margaret's welcome to the team "We are so proud of each and all of you. You've represented us to all in a manner reflecting the standards of Aquinas, educationally, athletically, and morally."
- The reflection of Championship team member Idelissa Lloveres '06, "Ms. Santos always said, 'Layups, free throws, and defense win the game.' And this is so true. But it was courage, persistence, and patience that made us the New York State Champions."
- The words of Coach Socorro Santos to her team, "Thank you for putting team first. You have overcome so much to become State Champions, because when it counted, you were one team. We prayed before every game, and then we shouted 'Together!' after the prayer. When we worked together as a team, no one could beat us."

The final prayer of blessing led by Sr. Catherine Rose was for the team, and surely included all these players, now and far, who have, through the years, gone out on the court for Aquinas. The New York State Champions are standing on their shoulders.

---

*An article in my high school newsletter about my team winning the 2006 NYS Division B Championship.*

# About the Author

Judith Brittany Wallace is a former student athlete from Rutgers University. As a pro, she played overseas for Dexia Namur Capitale in Namur, Belgium.

In addition to her work as a professional chef, Brittany is the CEO and Founder of Smiling Bellies Health Consulting, a premiere health and wellness education platform for serious and dedicated student athletes.

Smiling Bellies helps athletes build better body and self-awareness especially around mindfulness with food and beverage choices her client roster includes companies such as the American Heart Association, The Metropolitan Transportation Authority, the Health Care Foundation of the Oranges and Deutsche Bank.

Brittany grew up in the Bronx, New York but now resides in Middletown, NY with her family.

In her leisure time, she enjoys spending quality time with her husband, Austin, and son, Ray. Her other hobbies include spending time with family and friends, traveling, reading, fishing, playing sports and all things dealing with holistic and integrative health.

Made in the USA
Las Vegas, NV
03 June 2021